What the House Knows

Also by Diane Lockward

Poetry Collections
The Uneaten Carrots of Atonement
Temptation by Water
What Feeds Us
Eve's Red Dress

Craft Books
The Strategic Poet: Honing the Craft
The Practicing Poet: Writing Beyond the Basics
The Crafty Poet II: A Portable Workshop
The Crafty Poet: A Portable Workshop

Anthologies
A Constellation of Kisses
The Book of Donuts
The Doll Collection

Chapbooks
Greatest Hits
Eve Argues Against Perfection

What the House Knows

edited by Diane Lockward

Terrapin Books

Terrapin Books
4 Midvale Avenue
West Caldwell, NJ 07006

www.terrapinbooks.com

ISBN: 978-1-947896-78-9
Library of Congress Control Number: 2024951868

First Edition

Cover Design by Diane Lockward

for Ava
our sweet girl

Contents

A house is not a home unless it contains food and fire for the mind as well as the body.

—Benjamin Franklin

Wherever men have lived, there is a story to be told.

—Henry David Thoreau

Introduction

As a poet, I've often been asked where the ideas come from. As an anthologist, I've been asked the same question. The answer to both questions is the same: It begins with a haunting.

For years I'd been haunted by Ted Kooser's poem, "Abandoned Farmhouse." I was fascinated by both the poem's cold tone and its fierce attack on my heart. I also liked its appeal to my imagination with its carefully selected details, details that suggested a story, a story my imagination struggled to supply.

That haunting led to the idea for an anthology of poems about houses. After all, most of us have lived in one or more houses. I thought, too, about the variety of houses that might merit poems. And the variety of people and experiences inside those houses. As Thoreau suggests in one of this anthology's epigraphs, every house has a story to tell. And who doesn't love a story? The walls might not be able to speak, but the poets could.

Once the idea for the anthology crystallized, I put out a call for submissions, feeling fairly confident that I'd get a good response. I was not disappointed. In fact, the response was overwhelming. I received an astonishing 1,169 submissions, most including three poems.

In that pile of poems, I found the variety of houses I'd hoped for. Within the pages of this collection, you will find an old age home in Susan Aizenberg's "July at Rose Blumkin" and in Paulann Petersen's "At the Foster Home"; rented apartments in Ruth Stone's "The Cabbage" and Michael Waters' "Brooklyn Walk-Up"; a three-story house with a cedar closet in Therese Burns's "Cedar"; a schoolhouse in Ginny Lowe Connors' "Schoolhouse, 1820"; a house in the desert in Natalie Diaz's "If I Should Come Upon Your House Lonely in the West Texas Desert"; an outhouse in Jim Daniels' "The Holy Whispers"; and even a doghouse in Eric Nelson's "The Doghouse."

The poets also delivered on the emotional appeal I'd hoped for. Theodore Deppe's "The Singing" captures the fear parents feel when a phone call comes from an adult child in danger but so many miles away that the parents cannot help. Look at Susana Gonzales's spare but achingly beautiful "Open House." You won't be able to read that poem without wondering what happened within those walls. See also Jessica Goodfellow's "Torn," a poem that captures the destruction by fire of the speaker's childhood house, a real-life trauma also memorialized in the fiery YouTube video referenced in the poem.

You will also find here a number of poems about the people who once resided in the poem's house. The speaker in Beth Copeland's "Second Wife" feels her house haunted by the presence of her husband's first wife. Jennifer L. Freed's "When We Left the Hospital" captures the death of a brother as the speaker returns to the house that now holds only his memory. Maria Mazziotti Gillan's "The Little General" captures the house she grew up in with a devoted but uneducated mother. Recalling the death of that mother, the speaker feels around her "the warm arms that were the place // I call home." Sue Ellen Thompson's "The Empty House" captures an entire marital history with its griefs and joys and its people—the friends who came for dinner, a niece and a nephew, then a baby, and later an angry teenage daughter.

While I wanted poems that told stories and poems that pierced the heart, I also wanted poems that represented a variety of forms. Again, the poets delivered. You will find a range of architectural styles. Dina Elenbogen in "Duplex" offers a poem in that form. Saba Husain and Jeanne Marie Beaumont offer ghazals while Hailey Leithauser offers a villanelle. You will also find free verse poems, ekphrastic poems, rhymed and unrhymed poems, poems with and without punctuation, prose poems, poems in couplets and triplets, in quatrains, and in open forms.

As you move from poem to poem, from house to house, walk through the rooms known in Italy as *stanzas*. Listen to what the walls have to say.

—Diane Lockward

July at Rose Blumkin

—memory unit, Home for the Aged

Even this early in the morning,
heat breathes heavily against the panes
and the light's a white flame that warps
the glass of this picture window
overlooking the "wander garden"

and its border of young maples and beyond them—
I swear—gravestones rising

from the mist in the cemetery
just across the road. We've arrived
to find your father dozing here,
in the television room, deaf
to the chattering loop of *Lucy* reruns

flickering the big screen and the rhythmic
nonstop barking of the woman

slumped in the wheelchair
closest to it. At ninety-two, his skin's
almost translucent and his arms
are mottled with bruises the bitter
purple of ruined eggplants, and nearly

that large, a sorry map of needle sticks
and places where he's rested too long

against his walker. When he wakes
he knows us, but not our names,
what year it is, or how to call up sense
and syntax from the ruptured channels
harrowing his brain. Not all

he says is gibberish: *This is the shits,*
he tells us. *We're not doing this again.*

A man named Buddy, still dapper
in pressed jeans and a turtleneck, agrees.
Some daughter must do his laundry.
Mostly the men and women here
are incontinent, and like your father,

mostly they refuse to eat.
The young nurses are kind,

some of them lovely, as they crush pills
into applesauce for spoon-feeding,
offer juice boxes, and speak softly
to their charges, who doze
and nod, tremulous as dandelion puffs,

on the stalks of their necks.
It's hard to leave, and you give your father

your hand, tell him how many days
it will be until you return.
He repeats the number, *three,*
and seems to understand, and though all
his life he was a man uneasy

with affection, now bends
to kiss your fingers, courtly and sad.

—*Susan Aizenberg*

The House

In the beginning our house was a stone square. My father, an architect, added wings to accommodate our ever-expanding family. By the time I, the last child of six, arrived, it was shaped like a U. Children's bedrooms were on the two sides of the U so we could look out our windows and see each other getting dressed. "I see you naked," one sister would call out through an open window. Another yelled back, "I see you in your polka-dotted underpants!" From 7:00 to 8:50, I watched my sisters doing their homework, framed in the yellow light. At 9:00 sharp, the house went dark, the day ending with a flick of the switch—like a movie without credits. I lay back in bed and listened as the night sounds began: horses kicked their stall doors; tree frogs clung to the window screens and sang to one another; owls screeched and swooped over the fields, and the rooster crowed and crowed—my father always said that was because he was an Andalusian rooster and came from the wrong time zone.

—Nin Andrews

At First There Was No Air

then an evening breeze kicked up,
turning wild, so while I
waited for the nurse
to clock the time of death,
wind tore through the house,
curtains billowing, branches
banging against the screens
like anger, unleashed,
or grief. Or what?

What happens
in those long moments
after the heart stops beating,
before the mind quiets?

It's all I could think,
sitting on the hall floor
waiting for her body to be moved,
not wanting to close the house,
so whatever force remained
could free itself.

The nurse packed and left,
my sister driven away,
finally, in a black car,
as she had been decades earlier
the summer she was sent to camp.

Back then I had watched
from the front steps, as the car
turned from the driveway
and disappeared. She was gone
all summer. It was hot and rainy,
but by fall she'd come home.

—Cheryl Baldi

The Parable of the Burning House

—for Maxine Hong Kingston

We could have burned to death in our sleep,
my roommate says, then brightly asks will I drive her
to the edge of town to see the flames
bounding through grass and up eucalyptus trees,
each tree a torch that lights the next so it relays itself
across the landscape into the hills above our house,
a river of black smoke roiling overhead,
splitting the sky into blue halves.
We drive to the park, where a little crowd
watches blazes lope through the valley then leap
the freeway towards us like yellow lions.
I am still in my head, thinking of Heraclitus,
the fire philosopher, who says all things are made
of fire and will change back into fire,
but when a light voice asks, *Mommy, is our house*
going to burn down again? and a heat-blast
prickles our cheeks I shout, *Let's get out of here*
and we ricochet to the car in cartoonish fear.
It's easy to talk about the baptism of fire,
about the forge of the spirit, the purifying flame,
but when the sun is a bloodshot planet in the smoke
and the sky fills with orange nebulae,
people watching on porches start to run.
When we get home, my roommate packs and flees
but I'm on the roof with the garden hose
watering the house down as fire spills downhill
into the graveyard across the street, the trees like brushes
painting the sky red above the sleeping dead.
I'm gauging how much time I have
before I must run, too, when the wind shifts
and I stand on the roof with the limp hose, watching,
guilty, relieved, as other peoples' houses burn.
Here is a woman riding out of the hills on the handlebars

of a young man's bicycle while her house flames behind.
Wait, she says, *my novel is in the house.*
It is ten years' work, no other copies,
but the young man doesn't understand.
Don't worry, he says, *it's only things.*
California is burning and it makes the eye burn,
the nose burn, the tongue burn, and as the matter
of the world goes up it makes the mind burn as well,
since all things of the world are on fire, with the fire
of lust, fire of suffering, fire of attachment.
But it isn't easy to be a Buddha and let go
of the world that houses our things, the mind
that houses the world, of the women who loved me
for a while, of even these words for which
I've had such hopes. It isn't easy at all,
and even if it were, what would be the point of being
that free, of standing alone when the fires die,
like this bathtub on claw feet in black stubble,
this field of chimneys without houses?

—*Tony Barnstone*

Nobody Sees

I do not haunt. The house haunts me.
Often I am inside, but sometimes in the yard.
I never stray too far.
Sometimes I think I am in a dream,
or dreaming from far away, which means
I am asleep. The house sits on a hillside,
overlooks a valley I do not go down.
I move about the house. I don't
recall walking. There are always people inside.
People I love. They are alive.
That is why I do not believe I am dreaming.
For if I dreamt, the people in my dreams
would be those I once knew, would be dead.
It seems I have little or no control
of what goes or comes through the doors, that
I'm hardly regarded, like someone old.
But I am not old at all, though
restless, nor am I unhappy. I know
I need to be somewhere else, but where?
The house is in slow decay, the rooms
changing, colors fading, furniture
shifting, on the wall a painting
one moment, the next, a mirror.
The house needs repairs, but no one listens.
Which worries me. I want to save them
and the house, but everything keeps shifting,
like being on a sea no one else can see.
Like being the captain
of an interminably sinking ship
whose crew is under a spell,
strangely deaf.

—*Stuart Bartow*

Entering an Abandoned House

There is no electricity
in the porcelain spools
above jackknifed gutters
where three buzzards leer
like black question marks:
their version of see, speak and hear no evil,
their *Once upon a time* . . .

The door is thrown wide
on broken hinges. Batting
and Penzoil cans clot in the mud yard
among renegade clumps of daffodils
and snowdrops, trumpet vines,
viburnum gone haywire.
Corn mummifies in the bottom stubble.
The privy gapes.

The owl is at vespers.
His ironic *who* is second-sensed.
A spendthrift moon levitates.
The whippoorwill insists beyond count
that he is the whippoorwill.

Inside,
light on the dying wallpaper
eyes every tiptoe.
A half-eaten *Pilgrim's Progress*,
forty years overdrawn from the Anson Library,
sures a lame table.
A chair sits at its unfinished toil.
On the floor is an inch of chaff
and a heart-shaped mortuary fan, inscribed:
The spirit is willing,
but the flesh is weak.

Not a thing is prodigal here.
Abandonment has completed this house
and made mystery its intentions.
Like God,
it is inscrutable.

—*Joseph Bathanti*

The 101st Note on Violence

Cast iron: iconic. Romantic
even. Well oiled. Seasoned. But far
too heavy. Fatal. Certainly. If wielded.
Determination or luck.

Stainless steel. Core: aluminum.
Enlightened: even heat distribution.
Still, too much heft. Despite mass
production. Deceptive, the brushed metal shine.

Dollar store special. Surface: tin.
Or aluminum. Abandoned:
implicated: dementia. Dents
easily from a hardy scrub. It will do

nicely. For smacking my husband's
head. Emphasis or attention. Or defense.
Small injury. No lasting damage.
This is how I choose

a pan for the stir fry. Some minds.
The proximity (necessity, option)
of weapons. This is why. I plead (threaten).
No guns in the house.

—*Michele Battiste*

My Father's Houses

My father stands lean and young
in the formica kitchen, drinking a shot of Imperial.
He shoots his head back/swallows it all/
slams down the shot glass/turns around and says:
That's good stuff.

I still have the shooter
with a wild bull on the front that says:
Have a Snort!
He gave me the blueprint,
but my greedy heart wants more.

Every day he worked in the house
of the mill, making steel.
Every day returning to the house
on Skyland Drive, filling it with
the pain of fitting steel sheets.

When the house of my father's body left,
I watched and waited for him.
I said: *I don't want what's left
on the mountain.* I said:
What do you dream of now?

He hands me the map
to the house of dreaming:
*The buried treasure of you
is dying—you're watching so closely
that you're missing the world.*

—Jan Beatty

Summer Ghazal

The thieving humid air would seep in that house
In summer, time felt most to creep in that house

We wandered far into books, we whispered
Even in our games, we barely made a peep in that house

While father mowed the lawn and staked tomatoes up
The daughters learned to cook and sweep in that house

What was the tale untold? Why did a certain
Caller on the phone cause her to weep in that house?

The kettle's sung. Make up the bed tray—sugar, milk
& spoon, while you let the tea steep in that house

If you crossed the sixty summers and went back,
Think you could find the secret deep in that house?

A large fan purrs, drawn blinds blank the p.m. sun—
Cool sanctum of a room when she's asleep in that house

Do I exaggerate? Why does summer bring such gloom?
But how I loved the ones I keep in that house.

—Jeanne Marie Beaumont

In My Mother's Last Garden

The roses near the house have bloomed
and bloomed again.
The tomato vines are lush, laden
with fruit, sun-warm, red, taut with sweetness
and crisp green globes you will
slice thin, cornmeal coat, fry golden
and wrap in a fold of white bread.

The collard greens and cabbages are full grown,
though you will leave them to tender
with the first frost. Cucumbers secret themselves
on the other side of the neighbor's chain link fence
until your quick eye guides me.

Your eyes and ears are the only things quick about you now.
Cancer and age have leached your bones.

We sit on the small concrete patio where the sun rests
on your thin shoulders and a wind warm
as the remembrance of a Mississippi spring
soothes knuckles swollen with years and labor.

You lean close, your silvered hair scraped
into a single braid pinned
at your neck, and laughingly gossip
about the young man who bought the derelict
house next door, though you call hello and wish him well.

You won't come out here on your own, even
with your cane, you are so fearful of snakes.
And truly we may see one sunning itself
against the house once or twice a year.

When we lived in the small jumble of a house
just down the alley, you tended a patch
in a vacant lot hidden by weeds that towered

over your garden stakes.
There were surely snakes, but
you had children to feed and a sharp hoe.

You who made something from nothing
for so long, have a freezer full.

Now your garden runs
a slender path between the fence
and the concrete walk, filling every inch
with food that will feed us
when the world is frozen over again.
It will be long before a thaw.

—*Regina Berg*

Zero

First it was five above, then two,
then one morning just plain zero.
There was a strange thrill in saying it.
It's zero, I said,when you got up.
I was pouring your coffee
and suddenly the whole house made sense:
the roof, the walls, the little heat registers
rattling on the floor. Even the mortgage. Zero,
you said, still in your robe.
And you walked to the window and looked out
at the blanket of snow on the garden
where last summer you planted carrots
and radishes, sweet peas and onions,
and a tiny rainforest of tomatoes
in the hot delirium of June.
Yes, I said, with a certain grim finality,
staring at the white cap of snow on the barbecue grill
I'd neglected to put in the garage for winter.
And the radio says it could go lower.
I like that robe. It's white and shimmery,
and has a habit of falling open
unless you tie it just right.
This wasn't the barbarians at the gate.
It wasn't Carthage in flames, or even
the Donner Party. But it was zero, by God,
and the robe fell open.

—*George Bilgere*

No One Told Me About the Death

About the nest gone quiet under the roof.
The birds muzzled, eyes smeared shut
And an army of ants marching
Through their sockets, clasped like purses.

Muzzled birds, our eyes smeared shut.
As children, sometimes it felt like that.
Sockets clasped like purses,
Flying into the wired adult world.

It felt hopeless sometimes.
Even on Christmas morning
When wired, we'd fly to their adult world,
Eager to hatch our eggs, the ribbons and tinsel.

On Christmas morning,
They perched on the couch like two birds
And watched us hatch our ribbons and tinsel.
Mother fed us pie, father, seeds of grief.

Birds on a couch, a wire, they waited
To feel filled up
With more than pie and seeded grief.
We ate ourselves in silence.

Like birds muzzled, eyes filling up
The purses of our sockets
As armies of ants silently ate us
Under the roof of our nest gone quiet.

—Michelle Bitting

We Were Our Father's Second Family

Bright rectangles on the living room wall
where pictures must have hung,
we slept in their old rooms.
And outside the old homestead,

a black cast-iron hitching post
though we owned no horses; round white
millstones like giant moons held down
in the overgrown meadow.

Father's past in our present—
sometimes we'd sense it poking through
the gravelly chop of his voice—
the tall grass in the fields

bending toward it, the shadows
beneath the blades.

—*Sally Bliumis-Dunn*

Threshold

When the house was first ours
before it smelled of paint and wax
before we'd laid down rugs
or cooked a single meal
in its small outmoded kitchen

it had the stony scent
of shade under a garden shed
the damp unsettled smell
of quiet and disuse
though it hadn't stood empty

we'd open the back door
and there it was
intractable as loneliness
or the memory of loneliness
as if someone else's loss

were lodged within our gain
and it seemed important
it seems important now
that before we moved in
the house smelled stony

and shadowed even in the flare
of a mild November
as we crossed the threshold
ten twelve twenty times with tools
and tiles and cleaning supplies

each bright room blank
the walls and windows bare
steps uncarpeted floorboards scarred
but how sure I felt how safe
as if the history of this place

had always been leading
to the home we'd make
the home we were making
that strangely balmy fall
when a life seemed long

—*Jody Bolz*

I Needed for Months

I needed, for months after he died, to remember our rooms—
        some lit by the trivial, others ample

with an obscurity that comforted us: it hid our own darkness.
        So for months, duteous, I remembered:

rooms where friends lingered, rooms with our beds,
        with our books, rooms with curtains I sewed

from bright cottons. I remembered tables of laughter,
        a chipped bowl in early light, black

branches by a window, bowing toward night, & those rooms,
        too, in which we came together

to be away from all. & sometimes from ourselves:
        I remembered that, also.

But tonight—as I lean into the doorway to his room
        & stare at dusk settled there—

what I remember best is how, to throw my arms around his neck,
        I needed to stand on the tips of my toes.

—Laure-Anne Bosselaar

Good Housekeeping

She keeps trying to get her house in order
pretending with the rest of them
that the sun won't melt the earth,
that the seas won't burn, that the land
won't disappear under water or ice
or our own triggered destruction.
She keeps going back to the dishes,
to the meals, to washing the clothes,
to worrying over the state of the carpet
which is funny in a sad way
if you knew the state of her house—
the way the windows leak, the way the doors
have to be snugged closed, the way
they blow open anyway, with the slightest wind,
the cracks in the ceiling from settling or moisture
or just poor craftsmanship. She still decorates
for holidays, she still worries
over the tidiness of things, the nutrition of meals,
the state of the bathroom—of the toilet—
under assault by the misdirection
and lack of attention
of three males in one small house.
She is like some mad woman
straightening a frame during an earthquake,
righting a vase after a hurricane took off the roof.
She sees it is the season to behave so,
to live beside, within madness—
to mother through it.
It is despair pushed off
to vacuum anyway, to make a decent meal,
to require everyone to sit. She is hoping
the children won't notice or remember the windows,

the carpets—the way the door won't shut.
She is desperate for their happiness
for their solidity, for them to make it
to some new place
she never will.

                    —*Rebecca Brock*

Cedar

White and green-lawned and many-windowed,
the house we moved to in '64. That first day
we spun around the big rectangles of space,

the stairways endless. On the third floor
(a third floor!): two bedrooms, good sized, sunny.
A closet between the two. I opened it—

entered a forest of cedar and ember, a warmth
I'd never known in Flatbush. So fragrant
with musk, I felt a dizziness, lost in the house's

vastness, how a plant must feel in a pot too big,
roots loose and drowning. Hours passed,
and somebody found me there, smelling of pine

and pee and tears. Years later, I slept
with a boy in the sunnier bedroom, windows
looking out at the steakhouse where I waitressed.

When he left, I gathered the stained sheets,
buried them deep behind the cedar-scented coats,
the startled old fox that never shut its eyes.

—Theresa Burns

Feeling a little nostalgia for
a past that has never happened

—Hal Ackerman

My brother and I lived under the same roof, in the same house.
In the same house, my brother and I lived different lives

with different parents who kept our languages apart.
Languages apart, his part and mine: the bad boy, good girl, game of chance.

Whoever came to the party, rattled the windows with their voices downstairs.
With their voices downstairs, with different parents, no one sees you

in a game of chance, no one sees you in the hour of the never-sleeping.
Of the ever-sleeping, no one's child alone in each bed's boat is left unmoored

or sleeps unmoored in the dark's murmuring box of algorithms, the far-off
clang and ring of a buoy in a funeral of fog, nightlight obscured.

Obscured as a nightlight: the truth. Different truths, five years apart.
Five years apart, vexed in the next room, we both heard laughter split

the white wall between us in a wave, like only children can who can't sleep.
Of sleep in the next room, my brother and I yet harbored the same house.

—Elena Karina Byrne

Checkerboard Mesa

Dear mesa, dome of rock, do you remember your deep past? Vast seas, minerals pinwheeling through torrents, slabs sunk in silt? Do you remember giant clams, their ridged shells, a primordial fish buried to its globule marble eye? Mottled gravel carried by streams, dumped into your valley, layer after layer compressed & thrust by tectonic shifts? Remember ice spearing into your pores, wind whittling lines across your face, where now a few plants survive in summer scorch? Where now I lie, trying to remember my scant descent. A great grandmother's Yiddish name, the blue of my father's eyes, my mother's brown. Her smile before her memory-thieving disease. I can hardly remember my first home. Was my father really there? The after-that house built of stone (granite & sandstone, like you, mesa). Where five kids & our mother moved. The breakfast room, the dog waiting for gifts of liver & limp vegetables, slyly tossed. The backyard. The boy. Trees, rhododendron, grass, an abundance. Huckleberries in the nearby field, our buckets of plump fruit, its purple stain. The boy's pocketknife we used to prick our fingertips & mix our blood—a forever bond. (Have two kids done that here?) The beloved creek in front & back. Salamanders cupped in the boy's hand. In mine, a crayfish, its front claw brandishing air, desperate for something to grasp & hold. Like us back then. Like me, now. Searching for memories that slip away—like dirt falling between my fingers. A meager pile beside me, on top of you, immortal rock.

—*Robin Rosen Chang*

36 Myopia Road

—for the house where I might have grown up, in Winchester, MA

I cannot see past the houses lining
this street. Next door is 34
and across the street are odd
numbers. Overhead, pelicans fly
in search of seawater and fish,
or do I mean chimneys and storks?

An hour to Marblehead Lighthouse.
A house on the corner with a wide porch
finally sold. I imagined our family there
in future years. A red-headed girl named Ruth
never went to school. Always playing hopscotch.
I think of her as one-legged and blind.

A few houses wore rumors floating in air
around them. Someone said a cardboard box
of puppies had been buried alive.
A boy heard them whimpering all night
under fir trees that sighed. Next day
there wasn't a sign or any proof.

When my people left for the West Coast, an egg
in my mother's belly started to grow
into me. I can see the family sleeping
in fields as they crossed North and South
Dakota. Ripe apricots filched from trees,
field corn to break teeth on. Tomatoes, cukes.

Settling into the Puget Sound's salt air,
they awaited my birth like the Messiah.
Stars aligned and Magi came on horse-
and camel-back. Once, a blue and white
parakeet appeared in a pine tree. My mother
tried to catch it and then I was born.

I was afraid of deadly nightshade berries, *atropa belladonna*, plump in the bushes in a border near our house. Pretending to eat them, we'd gag, falling dead. We played rock school on the porch steps, banishing the witch, kickball in the street. Dusk coming down always made it look like home.

—*Patricia Clark*

Another Reason Why I Don't Keep a Gun in the House

The neighbors' dog will not stop barking.
He is barking the same high, rhythmic bark
that he barks every time they leave the house.
They must switch him on on their way out.

The neighbors' dog will not stop barking.
I close all the windows in the house
and put on a Beethoven symphony full blast
but I can still hear him muffled under the music,
barking, barking, barking,

and now I can see him sitting in the orchestra,
his head raised confidently as if Beethoven
had included a part for barking dog.

When the record finally ends he is still barking,
sitting there in the oboe section barking,
his eyes fixed on the conductor who is
entreating him with his baton

while the other musicians listen in respectful
silence to the famous barking dog solo,
that endless coda that first established
Beethoven as an innovative genius.

—*Billy Collins*

The Schoolhouse, 1820

In a small town in Connecticut, not far
from the river, a schoolhouse holds its breath,

door closed for a few weeks in autumn
so children can help with apple picking.

At dawn two does and a fawn lift their heads
from goldenrod edging the schoolyard,

retreat into the uncleared woods nearby.
A possum rustles into its den beneath the woodshed.

Inside the schoolhouse, whispers and recitations,
stories and small dramas linger like a dream.

That scratching sound could be Joseph or Charity
practicing penmanship, but it is not.

Only a few mice working bits of hay into their hidden nest
or foraging for seeds, for any crumbs that might

have spilled in the cloakroom, where one
forgotten lunch tin, labeled *Grant's Fine Tobacco*,

waits to be reclaimed. Double desks wait
in orderly rows, though they're ink-stained

and carved with crude inscriptions.
Gouged into one—*Hattie is a Pip.*

(Hattie left the school two years ago,
but a bit of her story remains.)

On the wall behind the teacher's desk
is a panel of wooden boards painted black,

clouded a little by words and numbers
incompletely erased. Not gone—

just waiting to reappear, on foolscap booklets,
in children's voices, or simply in minds, in memories.

—Ginny Lowe Connors

Second Wife

Fifteen years ago I drove south to see you as trees broke
into bloom—redbuds, pears, dogwoods—and my heart
unfolded like a bud closed too long in the cold.

Later, I moved into the log cabin built when you were
still married to a woman with chestnut hair that spilled
around her shoulders as she knelt in the dirt as if in

prayer, planting dozens of bulbs on the edge of woods.
Sometimes I wished we didn't live where her daffodils
burst yellow and green—worthy of Wordsworth's ode—

along a ditch beside the gravel road, a reminder of the life
you'd shared with her. I wished I'd never seen the wooden
box with recipes written in her hand on faded index cards—

Tomato and Basil Rigatoni, Amish Bread, Blueberry Cobbler—
and the wedding photographs stashed face-down in the drawer
of a bedside chest. I wished you'd never told me about the rugs

she wove on a loom in our bedroom. I wished she hadn't left
that green, down-filled vest from L.L. Bean in the hall closet.
It's not my style, I said when you offered it to me.

It looks like a life jacket. As I slipped it on, I hoped it wouldn't fit.
I was tired of living in a house with your ex-wife's ghost.
So sick of it! As I zipped it up, you said, *It's perfect.*

—Beth Copeland

The Holy Whispers

The stillness of Aunt Daisy's outhouse
nestled in a clump of trees out back
behind her tiny cottage near—
but not on—Lake Huron.

Our family's lot: to be near,
not on, though on stormy nights,
we could hear waves rage
crashing madly against shore.

The outhouse seat accommodated
Half-Uncle Hank's big ass.
His long sojourns in that small shed
left the boys to pee in the woods.

Daisy lost her first husband to a tractor
fire on their nearby farm
leaving her a widow with a daughter,
Cousin Beverly. Daisy and Henry

had no kids. God's will usually meant
something bad. A crucifix on the cottage wall
beside the starburst clock's loud ticking.
Aunt Daisy wore the same thin, faded housedress

every day of her life that wasn't Sunday.
What this boy remembers about sitting on the rim
of the outsized outhouse seat in the dark
is that it didn't smell as bad as what

the other kids said. All the shelter he'd need
was that small rickety box with the inside latch.
Toilet paper thin and wrinkled with dampness
but at least it wasn't a catalogue.

He was tired of cataloging his sins
in small boxes like that on the insides
of the church, the priceless shame
of mumbled penance.

Aunt Daisy sometimes carried
a rosary, jiggling it in her hand
like a pair of dice
though he never saw her pray.

In the close darkness he wiped
his ass and told no one his sins.
Outside, through that thin wall
he heard the lake's soft, gentle fizz.

Whatever the waves whispered
didn't have to be words.

—Jim Daniels

Not Here

—on the painting White Doors,
by Vilhelm Hammershoi (Denmark), 1905

Open rooms, open doors, doors
I walk through but do not find you.

Doors opening into openness,
the old/new space of I, not us.

And where is the window God
opens after shutting a door,

a window to the blue door of a sky
so wide no one can latch

or unlock it. The door to my heart
is also blue, a door opened

and stained blue before blue
was blue when it was only sky

and a door the dead walk through
if we give them a knob. So take

this knob, my knob, which unlike
yours still throbs, shutting, shutting,

shutting its small blue door
against this house, this labyrinth

of mute and open rooms.

—*Christina Daub*

Houses

You send me another one, at work, mid-morning, pixels
flying through the ether to form pictures of a life
five feet closer to perfect: emails that link to dream house
after dream house, each one more virtuous than the next,
at the beach, in the city, hidden in towns we've never heard of.
You don't tire of looking because what if it exists—
that single impossible find—like an undiscovered planet
in an infant universe spinning miles from the skittish
dogs next door, the cops stopped across the street again,
and the bleary-eyed woman, cigarette alight, whose racist slurs
fail to break the lawn guy. What if it's out there, far
from small-town stillness and suburban time?
The house we live in now, one hundred years old, sits
on stone, telling fortunes to the wind, whispering
sweet nothings we love but should ignore. Remember,
years ago, on the train ride out west, my hand warm
under yours, yours solid over mine as we sliced through the night,
shrinking valleys and mountains, searching. Remember
the births—a girl, then a boy—their tiny bodies like harbor lights
in the darkness of our room, signaling *this is home?* It's enough
and never enough. We all deserve a roof—of metal, wood, or clay—
but also something diaphanous that lets in moonlight
and distance, that serves up stars in their eternal shining. We're
always building houses, all of us, in our blood, in our lover's eyes,
real ones for shelter and metaphors to stretch out in as we run.

—*Heather L. Davis*

And Two Hydrox Cookies

Mom tells me Mom is upstairs cleaning the house.
Daddy's at work. Their imminent arrival gladdens.

I don't remind her both her parents are dead.
That would only bring fresh grief before

she forgets the loss all over again. I don't know.
Maybe Grandma is upstairs changing the sheets

or folding laundry. Maybe the subway will bring
Grandpa home soon. He will sit at the end

of the gray Formica table with a shot glass of schnapps
while Grandma simmers split pea soup and tongue.

Propped up in her bed, Mom sends the present to its room
without supper. Not enough cabinet space in the brain.

She's in an airplane, a cruise ship, a pleasant house
with cheery windows she's never been inside before.

A few years pass, and I've packed Mom away
with the rest of them. Look, she's sitting in the kitchen

next to Grandpa telling him about her day at school
between spoons full of soup before she can have dessert.

—*Jessica de Koninck*

The World Needs More Softness

Everything wants to live—gutter water
forming spears instead of falling,
the fire inside the house
of my heart crackling, the family

at the hearth of my valves, the spider
in the corner of the living
room spinning quietly.
The spider asks for little more

than an inch or so.
Even if I couldn't
see it, I'd still hate
knowing it was there.

You know this story.
I kill the spider.
I spread the flame, the arsonist
to my own burning building.

I'm the shrieking child
and the parent too shocked
to dial. The world needs more
softness and I weave in more

sorrow. I heard every tragedy
is a comedy given time.
Is that how it goes? Burial
doesn't stop the rot; even caskets

decompose. Not me, I won't
go slow, I incinerate
all things inside my home.
I cremate the hope, quiet

all screams. What a sight! Spines
of books that crumble to touch.
Here lies my heart among the ash.
I think I hear it writhe.

—*Claire Denson*

The Singing

That morning, two nuthatches sauntered head first down the pine
to a place where it was written in the wind, *Yes, they like it,*

and for that moment it was the house of the world,
the green bough where they chatted and strolled upside down.

Then our daughter called from Greece,
giving her first and last name as if to make sure

we knew who she was. Her four-thousand-miles-away voice
pleaded for help as a man hammered on heavy glass

and we thought we'd have to listen to each scream of her rape,
or murder. No. Neighbors intervened. We stayed on the phone

until a woman told us, *Stop worry. Please, stop worry.*
Alone again in our living room my wife said she felt *weak*

from the inside out, and I asked if she'd heard
something like a girl chanting the whole time. *There was this*

singing on the line, I said, but my wife hadn't heard it
and answered, *Do I have to start worrying about you now?*

I've never mentioned it again, it must have been some part of myself,
some knowledge that we can't, finally, keep each other safe.

Our daughter changed her ticket, crossed the night, and came home,
though what home is keeps changing since that call.

There is a map and a clock and a humming in the room,
there is coffee, or champagne and kofta curry,

there is a family, or at least the hope that someone might, if not
rescue us, hear us. There is this chatting together

as we amble about upside down and try to get used
to the perspective. And there is this shared time,

which is the green bough, for which I am grateful.

—*Theodore Deppe*

If I Should Come Upon Your House Lonely in the West Texas Desert

I will swing my lasso of headlights
across your front porch,

let it drop like a rope of knotted light
at your feet.

While I put the car in park,
you will tie and tighten the loop

of light around your waist—
and I will be there with the other end

wrapped three times
around my hips horned with loneliness.

Reel me in across the glow-throbbing sea
of greenthread, bluestem prickly poppy,

the white inflorescence of yucca bells,
up the dust-lit stairs into your arms.

If you say to me, *This is not your new house
but I am your new home,*

I will enter the door of your throat,
hang my last lariat in the hallway,

build my altar of best books on your bedside table,
turn the lamp on and off, on and off, on and off.

I will lie down in you.
Eat my meals at the red table of your heart.

Each steaming bowl will be, *Just right.*
I will eat it all up,

break all your chairs to pieces.
If I try running off into the deep-purpling scrub brush,

you will remind me,
There is nowhere to go if you are already here,

and pat your hand on your lap lighted
by the topazion lux of the moon through the window,

say, *Here, Love, sit here*—when I do,
I will say, *And here I still am.*

Until then, Where are you? What is your address?
I am hurting. I am riding the night

on a full tank of gas and my headlights
are reaching out for something.

—*Natalie Diaz*

Pleasure Harvest

When she took a position in a distant city, he knew
He could not follow, and in the months afterwards he built
Them a home where she was with him. Mornings
They made coffee, washed the berries, stood like normal
People in a kitchen, read books afterwards on a long couch,
Their legs touching in configuration, and one would interrupt
The other's reading to make some observation on the art
They both practiced. Afternoons he tried to work,
But the tales he composed were a collection of beginnings
And endings, characters with no mid-plots, Whisky helped.
Nights were difficult when her absence curled beside him,
A long-legged question no longer to be answered. So, why not
Try to sing of the pleasures of his drafty house, the overgrown yard,
His arguing children, the undisciplined dog, his ongoing work,
And she who lives outside his touch? When everything
Has shown itself imperfect, what else was there for him? Wisdom? Bliss?

—*Stuart Dischell*

To the new owners of 44 Brush Hill—

—what have you done to our blue door?
With three square panes
stacked up so every size of us
could look out and tell
who's ringing the bell—
anyone could look in and see
who we were—
our cement stoop sloping
to lawn lined by my father's leggy
shrubs under the huge plate glass
where my mother lit the tree—me—
outside that window—tossed up
to the sky by my father, an evergreen
v-neck, sister's red cape, brother's red boots—
our grass, December dead, mother's blurred
face behind glass, maternity dress—reindeer
decals flying the sleigh.

Where's our blue door, open in summer—
or the storm door I pushed—last to finish
my supper—rushing to capture the flag before dark—
the glass I pushed through. Stitches sewn—
my forearm shows no scar. Where is our plate glass
window birds flew into—beak down on our lawn
are they dead? No—as my mother predicted—
they got their wits back—flew away on their own.

Earth is wet, where our shrubs were.
Where I was tossed—and caught.

—Kelly DuMar

The Fire Responds to Questioning

Yes, I was there.

No, I did not call for help.

I don't know how I started.

What I remember is warming into being,
first my extremities, fingers of light
flickering, then only a gust of wind
and suddenly I was everywhere,
burning with hunger.

Linen drapes flared yellow
and glowed behind me.
Books smoked. A woolen armchair
sputtered orange while a pair of cranes
on a Chinese silk screen shrank from me,
smelling like charred meat.
The books blackened.

No, I didn't content myself with the library.
I spread out, made myself at home,
tried each bed, filled each dresser.

Understand, I hardly had time to think.
Someone dreamed me into life
and all I knew was doubling,
every thirty seconds doubling.

Tell me: what do you know
of how you began?
What did you burn as you grew?

—Lisken Van Pelt Dus

Duplex

—after Jericho Brown

52,470 Dead from Covid 19 in the US, March 19, 2021

A day leaves without closing the door.
The last shadows cleave to the blue awning.

Lost shadows dance along blue awnings
recalling the story of a yellow house.

In the story of the yellow dream house,
nothing bad had ever happened to anyone.

The house promised nothing to anyone
except rhyming words that appear in dreams.

Other-worldly voices whispered in dreams;
on waking the walls shook with aching silence.

How do you translate the aching silence
when it becomes a chorus of lost voices?

How do we bury so many lost voices—
when a day ends without closing.

—Dina Elenbogen

The House I Left Behind

was green. Its apple trees and roses
filled my mind. I turned the soil,
dug in coffee grounds and ashes,
let it burn into the blackest dirt.

A red blaze rose climbed the drainpipe
by the corner. On the cellar door, long arms
of ivy clutched their tendrils
in the white paint, the rusty latch.

And I left another house,
and another, and one more.
All of them were green.
There's another one, I think—

not yet happened, not yet left—
its windows wait
for light to come inside. This house—
the one I find, the one I might

be living in, the one I'll sweep and scrub,
the one I'll hammer and nail
with memories, the one behind me, before me,
the one that opens, the one that lets me in.

—Rebecca Ellis

The Second Offer

When I want to thaw out
my regrets I can drive
to the house we almost
bought together, exit
the car and descend that
steep hill of memory—
not the flowerless yard,
all rocks and dried weeds, stiff
against the gray shingles
and harsh glare of winter.
Instead, I contemplate
you circling the shade tree
we discovered out back
that April afternoon,
FOR SALE sign no longer
hammered into the lawn,
your hands darkened by dirt,
the prayer you whispered
among the heart-shaped leaves
and first sprouts of blood root
yarrow and chicory,
overgrown with desire,
what you'd do to the place—
contrite that I never
made a second offer.

—*Robert Fillman*

Command

Slow down and let the house come over you.
Let the walls stand and grow the same for you
as once they did. A house is not a show;
it happens more than once, if only once.
It opens. Then the long tides get their kill.
Come, make the shingles carry out the doors.
Make the roof part. The only house is yours.
And later, when the month has gone to years,
the heavy abstract house still will be yours,
coloring in the sun near these back doors,
here, where the grass, still loyal, mills its floors.

—Annie Finch

Ode

The edges of our books curl.

Mold grows on the bathtub caulking.

Too hot to make love, but not too hot to kill cockroaches,
scuttling along the baseboards.

No, we don't have AC except for a couple of window units.

(My friend, trying to get me to say what I like and what I
hate about Mississippi, said, "Well, one thing, you hate
living in a house without AC."

But though I've bitched about it for years, "Oh no," I replied,
"to tell the truth I love it, because it teaches me decay.")

And no, we don't spray, except for termites—about which
we have no choice, since we suffered from them seven
or eight times.

One May, when we drove home after school, we discovered a flock
of birds swooping and diving in the trees above our house.

When I went into the bathroom and looked out the window,
I saw a swarm of angels streaming from the outer bathroom
walls up into the light.

My God it was beautiful, a river of angels pouring from the transfigured
clapboards, and the birds snatching up this airy throng as it ascended— .

So that is my secret: how I love to be sunk in rifeness, in the itch and crawl and shimmer and seethe of flesh.

The heat tugs at me; it is the spirit's undertow, the riptide of remembering that we are, finally, helpless, borne out to sea, the prey of the mystery.

—Ann Fisher-Wirth

The Junk Drawer

The house admits it doesn't like the junk drawer
                              its pretense of importance like the narcissist's
casual affect its mindlike reserves of absurdity
                                        access the past and the house
is afraid of the past with its secreted shames and dreams you can hide there
                                        old lives old loves
among the single edge razor blades bells and plastic black spiders creep
out the house not so much when you shuffle picture hooks and stiffened
rubber bands or claw farther back
          to empty penny rolls loose pennies unblown birthday balloons
condensed and cramped to make room
            for newer glue sticks and twist ties but when you mindlessly
manifest the most inaccessible
                              stores of the drawer is an unedited diary
an elevated irrelevance of object and deny you keep
   doohickies sad as dry moist towelettes or eyeglasses without arms
chipped little teardrops for holding a mirror up to a wall
          in this drawer the past is naked as a button and as hopeful for closure
but how unimpoverishable you must think you are
                                        with a drawer like that
could prepare you for anything any sudden need
                          to sprinkle air through a jarless punctured lid
to roll the single die to live it all again to leave it to chance encounter
                the present memory of the wine tilted celebration
from which you saved this cork gone past
but at least you have the cork is something who knows which thing
will catch you off guard and take you
                          away from the house wonders if you save to be free
to forget or forget because you save
                                  each thing you hold onto simply
because it was there it was yours but the house doubts that you should

58

                              take prisoners hostage
now to then squirrel the hostile world of things
               combined to rubble rumbling in its sliding tracked
wooden box way to never
               make up your mind whether it serves or subtracts
to save the past as if from oblivion a waste
                                   land of the lost
thingamabobs paraphernalia of the parenthetical you hope you are not
                    yet the house has seen it all every defunct
appointment card pocket guide to your chakra
     energy centers tweezer and clothes pin and tomorrow will shift
six unsharpened monogrammed souvenir
     pencils perpendicular to the drawer and jam it shut for good

                    —Alice B. Fogel

House

—*after "Silently and Very Fast,"* by Catherynne M. Valente

I was a house once   very large   empty rooms aching like teeth
I knew what a house knows

of family genes in vast   mute   permutation   what it knows
of nature & nurture & cultural meme

tell me   how does this differ from love   I knew prison walls
that divide can also conduct a tapped code

& knew what a house knows of food—an egg yolk whisked into sherry
one very ripe peach   fire on stone

& still I starved & froze   I was outside on the inside   dark spar
of cypress   knot garden   boxwood maze

a web taut across any minus space   I was the silk & its spinner
& also her prey   I was the tremor

along each strand   its stressed silver resonance   the humming
beneath the precise surface tension of days

—*Rebecca Foust*

When We Left the Hospital

where my brother's body lay
in its stark white bed, it was three a.m.,
and we couldn't get into the parking garage
without asking the security guard
to buzz us in, and my sister-in-law was able
to say in a steady voice, *My husband
has died, and now I need to go home,*
and I thought how strong she was, how I
wouldn't have been able to speak
such words, and I was grateful
she'd been the one to say them and grateful
she'd married him in time
to carry him through these last two years
of scans and tests and trial drugs and more
trial drugs and grateful he'd fallen in love
before he died, and now
she was driving us to their home,
her steady hand on the wheel in the dark.
When she unlocked the front door, the air
felt still and strange. We drifted in. There, the piano.
There, the ticking clock. There the tufted pillow
on the floor. She gently touched his sweater,
tossed on the back of the couch, his open book,
his laptop sleeping beside it.
I looked at the neat line of medicines, useless
on the coffee table. Then we climbed the stairs.
We crawled into bed together, so tired,
after three days barely dozing
in hospital chairs, that we did not hesitate
about my sleeping in his place, and in the morning, the sun
drew us toward the window where, she said, he sat
in his last weeks, where there was space for his oxygen
tank next to the soft chair, and space for a tray
to hold the meals he could not keep down—

that first morning of the first days of sorting through
closets and shelves and files and finances,
we stood side by side and gazed
at the forsythia in full bloom,
and she told me, without turning her face toward mine,
that when she'd opened her eyes
to find the back of my gray head on the pillow
beside her, her first thought
was that it was his hair, that he was still there.

—*Jennifer L. Freed*

Depression Glass

It must have been October, right after
the annual hanging of the winter drapes
and the ceremonial unrolling of the rug
from its summer sleep behind the sofa.
Gone were the slipcovers, leaving
the upholstery stripped down to warm
arms again, and the little living room
transformed into a mother-hug of all
she labored for—the luxury of bastion
and snug, the thick stability of thick
pile, purchased with how many
on-her-knees hours of scour and rag.
The whir of the sewing machine at night,
and all those stretched nickels.

My sister would say this never happened,
or if it did, it wasn't this way, or if it was,
I never cried, or if I did, how could I—
so young—know what was to cry about.

A room like that, in the Snow White
haven of the dwarves' house, and I
no more than four, rowing a cardboard
box across the rug, its flowered sea
lapping at my hands that were my oars.
When suddenly, there was my father
dancing to the radio or some crazy song
of his own making, flapping his arms
and yawping like a great enchanted
gull of happiness having nothing to do
with me. Or her. And I saw as through
the glass layers of the sea what he'd
been before I came in my little boat
grinding its vast engines of responsibility,

dragging him under, changing him into
someone other than the drowned beloved
I'd be trying to make it up to all my life.

—*Alice Friman*

The Black House In Whitehouse, Ohio

Your life begins to end
when you mistakenly move
to Whitehouse, Ohio—
crossroad of flatland state-routes
where horizon becomes
a euphemism for desolation,
unlimited gray skies
under which the oak leaves
choose to grow upside-down.
Nothing holds your hand
like plain despair.
      This is
the perfect place to leave someone
for dead. Cornfields converge
the acres into miles in all directions.
The occasional bald clearing
of a farmhouse or barnyard
where old widows plot
the next morning's chores
and crimes.
      You thought
you were getting away,
from the city-glare and traffic-
rumble. Instead, you tend to
a broken red tractor
in the sagging barn out back—
losing one shingle, one board
at a time—and every night
the badgers come out to murder
what scurries in the otherwise
quiet country dark.

—*Timothy Geiger*

The Little General

My brother called our mother "the little general"
when we were teenagers, my brother driving

the car, my mother sitting next to him, her head
a small dark knob barely reaching the top of the seat,

my bossy mother who told us how to live our lives,
my mother who was always moving. When I

remember her, I see her almost as a blur,
like the cartoon of the road runner, my mother

who washed all the dishes as soon as the last bite
of food vanished from the plate, my mother who held

my doctor brother's foot until he fell asleep when he
was still a boy, my mother who sat at the kitchen table

with us, always ready to hear the stories of our lives,
ready to tell the story of hers, my mother who told me

everything that was wrong with me so I still hear her voice
though she said she told me for my own good,

my mother who loved the feel of the earth on her hands,
who smelled of flour and spices, who baked

thousands of loaves of bread, cooked innumerable
fragrant meals for her children and grandchildren

in the basement kitchen, my mother who taught me
how to laugh, my mother who could not read and write,

and although she wanted to go to school, my father
wouldn't let her, "Women don't need to go to school," he said,

my mother who did not know how much money my father
had in the bank and never wrote a check,

my mother who wanted to learn how to do
everything, my mother who could quote poems

she memorized in third grade in Italy before
she had to leave school, my mother who drew

an imaginary line around us to keep us close,
the front stoop our boundary, the family country,

her little sturdy body better than any magic charm,
my mother whose skin turned orange before

she died, though the week before she got sick,
she planted a huge garden. We were sure

she was too powerful to die. Ma, even now,
ten years after the funeral procession led us

to Calvary Cemetery and to the mausoleum drawer
they filed you in, I wish I could drive over

to your house and find you there, your earthly humor,
your warm arms that were the place

I call home.

—*Maria Mazziotti Gillan*

Open House

On Sunday afternoons strangers parade through my home
like people passing a car wreck,

greedy eyes ogling over what lies inside
with no regard for the sorrowful state of the victim

who was blindsided by the breakup,
the screeching end of love.

I am ashamed to be lying here in the road
with my insides out for all to witness.

—Susana Gonzales

Torn

Time makes a voodoo
doll of my body.

With its ten thousand needles
sharp as second hands,

time pricks my skin, pokes
my viscera, trying to get at my mind's

velvet archive of cottonwoods
and cottonmouths. Memory is

a shifting shoreline,
ragged as an envelope torn open,

spilling out what had been sealed away.
Time's two longest needles, past and future,

click against each other as they knit a filigree,
the net of the now I am caught in,

waiting to be cast off, finished, torn closed.
Instead, I'm torn open again, this time

by a video on YouTube, a firefighters' training
film, footage in which my childhood home burns

down, over and over, in a flash-
over that started in the family

room. Again I watch, and again. It is good
practice. Even in the final frame, so much smoke.

—*Jessica Goodfellow*

My Father Put Out

Somehow the wires of memory
must have jiggled together
for a night, or maybe some
homing instinct has outshouted
jumbled noises of his mind—
and here he comes, wobbly
but determined, and no nurse
in sight. He's headed home
to the apartment my mother
put him out of just a week ago.

Eloping, they call it, one
of the more accurate euphemisms,
I think, as Dad yearns
with weedy stubbornness
toward the marriage bed
he's known for fifty-five years.

So he's heading home,
the uninvited dinner guest,
my prodigal father come for
his keys and a nap in his chair.

And not mad at us, exactly,
where we sit startled
over our pasta and wine,
just irritated in general
as if at a traffic jam
or hammered fingernail.

He stands in his study a good
long time, picking up padlocks,
shuffling letters, grabbing
a pen knife like a guilty sweet.

How to tell him so he understands
you can't be here? Not in
his new life, not when he tilts
and wanders, pitches and falls,
forgets to dress for a walk,
forgets undressing before a shower.

Still he remembers how a fever
would always break,
bone and skin knit,
key slip properly back
into its lock. Never before
was he so put out, having
to sneak back into our banquet
like child or thief.

—*David Graham*

Cricket in the House

Not the music. Like a bicycle bell
ringing faster as you pedal faster.
Not the spring-set contraption
of its body, which I expected to be big
as a mantis, but could sit comfortably
on a nickel. No, not in the half light,
how its trilling turns the room
into a field at dusk in which someone's
set a couch, a coffee table, a wingback.
And not transformations generally:
sound making space like the time I busted
an eardrum and brought, to the silence
of my bedroom, the shushing of a distant
ocean. Not like that. And not
how it got in. Or how long it would be
until and why it would die. Just what
do they eat and drink, anyway?
                                    But
the thought of music meant for others
of its kind now backed behind a couch
on hardwoods, antiseptic and dry—
a patina of dust, cobwebs
at the legs, and cat-hair tumbleweeds
as I cross the room and it falls silent,
the cricket, briefly. And how it must
long for mud and coolness, for the dew
night covers everything with, for all
the other sounds insects make that
I don't notice but that it notices, how
it must register dislocation, even
isolation, and how none of this
alters its quality of song.

—*Benjamin S. Grossberg*

Ode on Paradis and the Longing
for a Place that Never Was

My sister and I are talking about our childhoods,
    which have the same cast of characters, but differ
so much that it's hard to believe we shared a bedroom
    for so long, and she often recounts how I threw up
on her, which I don't remember and neither did our mother,
    but my sister believes it so it's part of her story
but not mine, and I'm the only one who remembers our parents
    being in love or living in France in a little village in Alsace
called *Paradis*, and on our honeymoon, my husband and I
    drove through but I couldn't find the house, and twenty
years later, my mother and I made the same trip, and she
    couldn't remember where the house was either,
until she recalled a man who'd walk by every afternoon
    and urinate right across the street from our house,
which was kind of weird, but there was a lot of anti-American
    feeling, and when my mother remembered the guy peeing
that led us to the house, *toot sweet*, as she would say
    in years to come, along with *mangez*, the only French
she picked up, and our French landlords didn't want children
    in their fancy parlor but made one exception at Christmas,
and my mother created one of her magical holidays with a tree
    that dazzled, and my sister does remember how December
was a gorgeous time though she doesn't remember that one
    or the snow piled high, or how cold it was all year,
and when I think of that time, the Welsh word *hiraeth*
    comes to mind, or the longing for a place that never was,
and maybe that's what *Paradis* was, with fresh baguettes
    delivered every morning with milk and cheese,
and my mother so young and pretty, and there was a fireplace
    in the room next to the kitchen, where she fried chicken
and made pot roasts, and she would call us in from play
    with, *Mangez, kids*, which my sister remembers
from three years later in Virginia, De Gaulle having kicked us out

of France because according to my mother America
wouldn't share the nuclear secrets with the French,
        and that's a big secret to share I'll grant you,
and France had just come through two wars which messed up
        the landscape, but time has healed those wounds,
and you see a lot of nuclear power plants, too, so someone
        let those secrets slip, and sometimes I wonder
if *Paradis* even existed, because my mother and father
        are both dead, and I'm the only one left
who remembers my mother slathering those baguettes
        with peanut butter no French child would ever eat,
and the little picnic place with merry-go-rounds in the water
        of the lake, and when my husband asked a man
who lived in Paradis about our landlord either Monsieur Iray
        or Siray, because my parents had forgotten, he said,
No Americans ever lived here, so now I'm thinking it was all
        a dream of paradise that my little girl's heart
made up out of nothing, even my young parents in love
        with each other and the fire in the dark cave of their hearts.

—*Barbara Hamby*

Inauguration of a House

Right away the ill omens begin:
the seller's lawyer has a blood-stained eye.
Then a drunk driver knocks the mailbox down,
and I kill a snake in the basement,
its mottled body writhing on the slab.
All before we've even moved in.

Is this an initiation? We try to dispel any evil
by sprinkling kosher salt in all the corners,
then set to work to make the house
our own. All the old knob-and-tube wiring
is ripped out of the horsehair walls
and replaced with virgin Romex.

I spackle and repaint, bash my knuckles
lugging boxes in, struggle with molly
and toggle bolts, and pinch my thumb with pliers,
raising a blister as dark as a Concord grape.
The plumber gets our one toilet running
but warns, "She's going to sweat like a pig."

The house doesn't begin to feel like ours
until we're making love in it, on this bed
we had to dismantle to get upstairs,
and under this roof that needs repairs.
We're trying not to think about that now,
making sure instead that this is good

for both of us, making it last,
tasting the wet salt on each other's skin,
here among these boxes stacked
like sandbags against disaster or attack,
until these walls I've patched
absorb our cries and take us in.

—*Jeffrey Harrison*

[Things the realtor will
not tell the new owner]

When she left she left so many ghosts the whole place is

poisoned with them their stray sadnesses untraceable scents

those cold holes in the very air so when you wake your throat

choked with tears having dreamt some strange some other

beloved you never knew and know is gone and this morning

desperately miss don't panic please please rise instead into

the groundmist walk out among her patient anchored trees

her ghostbear is there but will offer no harm will pace hungry

wary and finally away there too the ghost coyotes who filled

her nights with difficult with strange music you'll hear her

ghostbirds the hawk as a tiny falling wind the owls of winter

dying like prayers the morning flight of songbirds who carve

her shape into the yard with their swerving whose young

are born into the feel and smell of her hair rise and walk

through all of it to the lake next door you'll find her spot

on shore you'll let those borrowed those inherited tears

join hers the ones she shed so long ago you'll let small fish

rise to the drops salted and falling it will all feel familiar to them and like she's come home so go about your days

in phantom pain as if your own life had been badly amputated

then badly sewn back but when you weary of it slip

into that room ease down on the bed the one she left

and left and left again when you lie down you choose the other

side you sleep in sleep your arm reaches to where her back

once curved you pull her impossibly toward you nest rest

like that but wherever it is she is she and all her creatures

sleep on uncomforted and alone

—*Leslie Harrison*

3rd Avenue North, Seattle

Look, Dear Heart, it's me
in winter cap and coat,
dressed, for once, for weather,
posed in front of the old apartment
where we were always cold
and often hungry. Meager haunt
of sauce-less spaghetti,
of peanut-butter and day-old bread.
You were a student here, studying
into the night while I read novels
and felt abandoned and unloved.
Sundays, I bawled on the phone
to Mother and you called your dad
to talk sports, laugh about my cooking.
Here is where I lay on the sofa
aflame with fever, where a punk
intruder punched your front teeth loose.
Here is where we fought every day,
made love every night.
Here is where we brought
our first two babies home.
Here is where we mapped
our sparkling future.
Here is where we couldn't wait to flee.
Now, the babies are grown
and you, Dear Heart, are gone.
But, you would recognize this place,
it's just as we left it—
the faded paint, the splintered door
opening to the asphalt lot.

—*Donna Hilbert*

Kitchen Shrine

O blessed Madonna of perpetual
kitchen reconstruction, in your name we pray
that all our contractors may be punctual
and sober, that lines on each marbled gray
piece of countertop align at crucial
corners, that cabinets open the right way
and are actually made of real maple
and not just overpriced cheap laminate.

Protect us from appliance temptation
insomuch as it exceeds our budget.
Let us rejoice in less illumination
than what we had agreed when we discussed it
with the first or second electrician.
Let water leak with grace into a bucket.

Bless us, this day, with silent refrigeration,
and marriage that survives this renovation.

—Cindy Ellen Hill

Living Room

In the cave of memory my father
crawls now, his small carbide light
fixed to his forehead, his kneepads
so worn from the journey they're barely
useful, but he adjusts them
again and again. Sometimes
he arches up, stands, reaches, measures
himself against the wayward height
of the ceiling, which in this part of the cave
is at best uneven. He often hits his head.
Other times he suddenly
stoops, winces, calls out a name,
sometimes the pet name he had
for my long-dead mother
or the name he called his own.

That's when my stepmother tries
to call him back. *Honeyman*, she says,
one hand on his cheek, the other
his shoulder, settling him
into the one chair he sometimes stays in.

There are days she discovers him
curled beneath the baby grand,
and she's learned to lie down with him.
I am here, she says, her body caved
against this man who every day
deserts her. *Bats*, he says, or maybe,
field glasses. Perhaps he's back
in France, 1944, she doesn't know.
But soon he's up again on his knees,
shushing her, checking his headlamp,
adjusting his kneepads, and she rises
to her own knees, she doesn't know

what else to do, the two of them
explorers, one whose thinning
pin of light leads them, making
their slow way through this room
named for the living.

—*Andrea Hollander*

This Is the House in Which I Am Lonely

In which I am untouched—it's snowing,
someone says it looks like the house
from a movie about the holidays.
A story about someone returning,
then, likely from a great distance
or after a long time. These are
the only stories in the world.
Escape the cyclops, cross the seas,
it's still snowing, I'm home,
even when the stars are behind the clouds,
as now, some light gets through —
words are not the same as touch,
a postcard is not a vacation,
the way you know your life is not a story
is that stories have shape
and in stories desire has purpose.
This is the body in which I am lonely—
what if it's loneliness that keeps me alive.

—*Amorak Huey*

Resisting the Ghazal: House

Remember spruce, pine, fir, sunlight slanting on upright timbers
We trespassed on bones, believing all along it was a forest

Not a fraction of how it was like for those on the inside: post, and beam
A colossal untethering of the utterly personal, the unbearable

They never left those rooms. Murk blurred the living from the half-living
A desperateness to be. Anywhere but the present. Indelible sorrow

Tent cities that arose, unromantic blips built on the backs of constructed lies
On the backs of our countertops, hardware, flooring, custom windows

The ghazal never came, though the refrain was repeated in every house
You thought a rose would bloom in the aftermath, Saba, not even a weed.

—Saba Husain

Ice Fishing, Lac Qui Parle

At night light shines in the houses
on ice. Our fathers silently
hunch over mouths of dark water,
wait for silver fish to flash
in the black just below them.
In the blackness surrounding, the sky
lets go of its snow. I think of the houses
as lanterns, or words
that rise in the throat.

Weeks ago, when they were certain
the lake had frozen
beyond melting, they
hauled their houses onto the ice,
dragging them like lives
they longed to inhabit. How far

away from them we wait
in lit kitchens. Listen,
there are words that simmer in us
like liquid, almost soundless. Soup on the stove,
steam rising to the slanted ceiling. Lost
drops gather there and fall
to stream the frigid windows.

At night the wind is fierce
enough to bend the rigid pines
and drown the sounds of dark
longing, the hunger that pulls
weaving bodies to the surface,
mouths open, shaken fins
flinging drops of water,
silver in the fire.

—*Alison Jarvis*

Nine Month Lease

I was the last of five to rent the same womb.
The eldest, sister Linda, broke the place in
when the walls were still shiny and slick.
She put up some drapes and made it a home,
adding a fine leather chair and books
on opera and Tuscany. Judy came along
a few years later, kind and gentle in her ways.
She wrapped herself in a long cotton shawl
and mixed drinks with cinnamon and cloves.
Brother Jim soon followed, the musical one,
and left his records and radio playing all day.
The last boarder, Joe, a painter at heart,
left a finger-paint mural and some of his art.
By the time I arrived and the lease was signed,
the womb had been vacant for seven long years.
I hadn't yet known those who'd lived there before,
but beneath the fertile layer of dust
I discovered the things they left behind:
well worn leather, soft warm cotton,
songs never heard and colors never imagined.
With little to do but wait, I settled into the chair
and draped the shawl over my lap,
set the radio to Bach's cello Suite No. 1 in G Major
and became lost in the dazzling color and flow
of the mural before me, all the while
not knowing the shape my life would take
when the lease was up and I found myself
out on the street.

—*Jeffrey N. Johnson*

The Poet Leaves Muzot for Paris and the Housekeeper Remains

Muzot could get so cold in winter
that Rilke's breath froze on his pillow.
       —Brigitte Duvillard, Foundation Rilke

I climb the narrow stairs and open the door.
You know how it is, the way the departed leave

a souvenir in the shuttered room. Just a wick
of memory and then his roses. Petals

spilled across his thick duvet,
yellowed as the pages of my bible.

I crawl inside the place most forbidden,
pull back the stiff sheets and slip inside.

This bed is only big enough for one body.
This moon is only bright enough to cast

this anchoress' shadow. I know I am best loved
in the arms of winter where I can't see

the edge that separates me from a blind sky.
I disappear in a fine powder of solitude without

need to share my loneliness.
Because he's asked me to wait again, I will.

I will wait to see him arrive—wind walking
in white spats on the frozen road.

                    —Lois P. Jones

When I Become Your House

I'll shawl myself with wrap-around porches,
adorn myself with a pined-for third-floor balcony,
let the wide view in through diamond-paned windows.

I will keep you safe from that high western wind
that blows ticks off of tomcats. I'll protect your cards
for cribbage, I'll hold the hearth for Red Pajamas Night,

when we can all sleep close. I'll plant bulbs in the fall
for spring flowers, seeds in the spring for fall food,
then hollow out dim space where the baby can laugh

in her sleep. I'll be the scent of water to returning
salmon, you, our son, our daughter. Your champagne
corks will dimple my ceilings every last birthday.

I'll be beginning and end of dog walks, bike rides,
road trips, anchor for the few blest decades we get.

—*Tina Kelley*

Anything with Wings

The day I sold our family house, I closed
and locked the door and walked away. Never
curious to see what the new owner would do
with the only home of my childhood, I have no idea
what happened to it, no idea if anything was left
in some dark corner or on the hidden staircase
closed off in the emptiness of my mother's closet.

That life, as I knew it, was gone years before I
let it go—a stippled history of secrets and sadness—
dreams that lingered but couldn't come true.
As a child inside that past, I believed in anything
with wings—haloed angels, birds with feathers like
crested sunlight, and moths that fluttered dust
on my hands when I touched them.

In the woods across the street (by the pond where
wild ducks came each autumn), my cousin Eddie
found a space where starlight sifted through
darkness and traced our faces—a quarter moon
cloud-ribbed high above the trees. We didn't know
how time would change us, if anything might remain
the same—the essence of us still there; phantoms
of the old house, apparitions in whatever is left
of the forest, forever wandering the lost road home.

—*Adele Kenny*

Finding a Long Gray Hair

I scrub the long floorboards
in the kitchen, repeating
the motions of other women
who have lived in this house.
And when I find a long gray hair
floating in the pail,
I feel my life added to theirs.

—*Jane Kenyon*

My Father's House

I was one of the black-hearted ones, my father said,
a Protestant whom they would try to proselytize,
thumping his dictionary like the Bible it was
to him, warning me not to be seduced by the robes
and glories, the incense and beautiful words.
But the gold and smoke, the brocade, the murmurs
as penitents knocked at their hearts to open
the door to mercy, forgiveness — who could resist
such pageantry? The chapel walls were painted mauve
and during Lent, with all the saints and the Virgin
draped in purple cloth, it seemed some elaborate
fashion show was about to begin. Heretical
to think, my father said. No doubt the nuns saw
my dereliction [*more thumping*] and were contriving
immediate conversion. I was not to let my guard down.

But God was my guard, and the hosts of angels
ready to descend and save my wayward soul,
I would think on my way to school, bantering
like a normal girl on the five-mile bus ride
but all the while thinking this might be the day
the chapel wall opened and Christ stepped through
in a blaze of light to save me, and everybody
would see, and fame would come, and the dirt
floor under the sofa where I sat while my father
explained the world would vanish into carpet,
walls, heat: the finished house of my father.

But my father's house was all words. Make a bed
of words to lie down in. Make a floor of words
to stand on. Make a faith of words that nothing
would betray—not his drunken promises,
not his blueprints untouched under ash and dust.
Make a hope of words, the start of forgiving.

—*Lynne Knight*

Abandoned Farmhouse

He was a big man, says the size of his shoes
on a pile of broken dishes by the house;
a tall man too, says the length of the bed
in an upstairs room; and a good, God-fearing man,
says the Bible with a broken back
on the floor below the window, dusty with sun;
but not a man for farming, say the fields
cluttered with boulders and the leaky barn.

A woman lived with him, says the bedroom wall
papered with lilacs and the kitchen shelves
covered with oilcloth, and they had a child,
says the sandbox made from a tractor tire.
Money was scarce, say the jars of plum preserves
and canned tomatoes sealed in the cellar hole.
And the winters cold, say the rags in the window frames.
It was lonely here, says the narrow country road.

Something went wrong, says the empty house
in the weed-choked yard. Stones in the fields
say he was not a farmer; the still-sealed jars
in the cellar say she left in a nervous haste.
And the child? Its toys are strewn in the yard
like branches after a storm—a rubber cow,
a rusty tractor with a broken plow,
a doll in overalls. Something went wrong, they say.

—Ted Kooser

When you've lived in a house for fifty years,

it breathes with you in your sleep;
it lights your lucky way
from morning bed to kitchen
of blessings–the filled
pantry, the humming fridge
committed to keeping the berries
you love for breakfast
firm and delicious.

It lets you move freely through
its pleasant rooms, as you water your
peace lilies and philodendrons,
and after a slightly scary check-up
at the doctor's, and some fill-in shopping,
welcomes you again for dinner
and a little non-alarming TV, watched
with your spouse from the soft settee.
It vouchsafes both of you
a quiet passage to untroubled dreams,
guarded as it is by ancestors
assembled in multiple albums
in its cabinets, pressed
against each other in phalanxes.

You want to pray to this house's
lares and penates. You want to
beg them to never let you
leave it, never make you sort
the dust-encrusted plastic bins
entrusted with hundreds of letters
you and your husband wrote to each other
in an almost mythical past.

You want to entreat the household gods
to keep them forever reachable
and uncorrupted on their sagging shelf
in the garage of inexhaustible mysteries.

—*Judy Kronenfeld*

Going and Staying Home

—Uzès

The city has been making improvements
in the Parc du Duché: a new playground
for children, exercise machines for *les sportifs*,
tables with inlaid boards. Someone has set out
white pebbles and chestnuts for a game
of chess or checkers. Is this what it means to live
in a particular place, to belong here: watching
day by day as this small world is renewed,
till the barriers come down and I start a game
with my husband? (He always wins.)
To know the answer when visitors ask
where to find the Roman aqueduct? To prefer
Le Pêcher Mignon for pastries, La Nougatine
for bread?

   Soon I will leave, return
to another city where I know the walking paths,
which gardens have yellow aconite in February
or bee balm and echinacea in high summer, asters
and autumn-blooming clematis. Where I buy bread
at Phlour, shortbreads at Bittersweet.

     Some homes
I can no longer reach except in fragments
of memory: the little white house where my mother
planted tulips, the apartment at 101st and West End,
the new-built house, now more than fifty years old,
on a dirt road leading to a farm whose cows
liked to wander. The farm must be gone,
a sub-division in its pasture. A slippery word, home,

though I always thought it marked the foundation,
the magnet to pull me back. I live now between
two poles, always going and coming, packing
and unpacking; always hovering between stop
and start over.

—*Susanna Lang*

In My Last Past Life

In my last past life I had a nut brown wife,
a gray and white house looking over the sea,
a forest for love and a river for grief,

a lantern for hope, for courage, a knife,
a city for distance, lights spread on the sea.
In my last past life I had a brown wife

subtle and busy and contented and brief,
(she stood in the dusk silhouette with the sea)
a forest and love and a river, and grief

was a ghost hidden green in the leaves,
an echo off cliffs that bound back the sea.
In my life it would last, my past and my wife,

the wren in the garden, the moon on the roof,
day winds that flirted and teased at the sea,
the forest that loved and the river that grieved

the life that was garden and day wind and thief
(each sunrise and sundown the turn of the sea)
the life that I had, and my last brown wife,
a forest for love, a still river for grief.

—*Hailey Leithauser*

Earth/Body/Home

In the same year
      that I made a human

my husband embarked on
      the greatest journey of his
      young, capable life.

The year I built
an extra set of
      bones and teeth
      a second heart
      arranging them
      into a breathing body

he assembled glass
slices of wood
pillars and beams
into a house.

    While he made a home,
        I *was* a home.
When I was done being a home,
        he provided one.

I know no greater examples
of craftsmanship than these.

        The journey took him one year
        and me just short of nine months

for us to go from container
        to container

each building a masterpiece
from our own fluids
in our own ways,

      every square inch
      utter perfection.

This is what it meant
      to be partners.

We were water
      pouring into each other

      taking turns
         doing the holding.

Meanwhile the Earth
      is mother to all mothers
      simultaneously,

      forever holding us.

This is what it means to be
      children

      together.

—*Svetlana Litvinchuk*

Memory of the Real Estate Collapse

the night the kitchen
    plummeted into my bedroom
        I awoke in the dark just before

water trickling in the walls
    like wicked laughter
        the skylights leaked a torrent

plumbing conspired a tsunami tide
    I lay still and pulled
        the comforter to my chin

kitchen sink cratered
    at the foot of the bed
        kneeling like a sacrifice

fridge tumbled, pantry spilled
    its ribbed cans of guts
        stove and microwave piled on

through the hole overhead
    I gazed to the little
        window that a moment before

framed the sink like an escape
    hatch—with yes the moon full
        bright with deflected light—

a muddy finger rang
    the doorbell on the porch
        landslide cackled too big to fail

dragged from the remnants of home
    I tumbled down
        the liquid hillside drenched in gloaming

—Eric Lochridge

Still Life of House in Late March

A century old, she knows
how to pose, shutters not even twitching
in natural light as the artist tinkers
with perception, vandalizes the stark air
with voyeurism. She is naked
of snow, leaves, flowers
but beautiful in her simple stance
among curved hills.

Maybe her weathered
boards will creak onto canvas
or a swallow peep through the brushstrokes
where a nest clogs a slanting chimney.
She is not saying, obedient
to the solemn man now sketching
wrinkles across her face,
re-constructing shadows
of memory,

while beyond his vision,
I'm sure she daydreams of us
who are watching inside,
forever waiting to see
what she will tell of our lives still
moving and moving.

—*Marjorie Maddox*

The Occupant Imagines
the House as a Great Fish

It has already swallowed a century, each year a silver iridescent
   scale. For eight, she has lived in its belly,
slightly beyond her means. How well she knows its creaks and
   currents of air, its slow, digestive rhythms.
How many mornings she has stood behind the large, glassy eyes
   that stare impassively down on the park,
observing the junkies and dog walkers awash in airy sunlight; and
   how many evenings felt herself sinking
incrementally into the still and liquid night.

Sometimes she imagines the former occupants: the long dead
   whose bones are coral, or the others—dense
spirits skimming the surface in narrow boats. She'd like to ask
   them a few things. *Why did you wallpaper the
ceiling? Do you grieve for your body?* But their words, dissolved in
   air, can find no purchase here, and she is not
yet proficient in the dialects of silence.

Still, there is no ill will. They come, untenable shadows, and go,
   stirring the boughs of tall firs. Today too the
sun appears; birds call across the surface of the morning. *Song of
   dissolution, song of light.* She turns from the
window as the thought rises—*the house is a fish, and I*—then
   glides into shadow, softly as the back door
opening, closing.

—*Jennifer Maier*

Renovation

Survey, apply, bid, borrow,
sign. Then we shifted all
we had from room to room, nightly
wiping dust that sifted out

of each day's progress. On the plywood
wall dividing old from new
we lined our two small boys, backs flat
as if to face a firing squad,

then outlined them in markers. Until
the workers tore it down, their shapes
stood still in time, superintending
the come and go of builders with

their coffee cups and power tools.
The house came true, the phantom boys
came down and grew, and in the rooms
wide enough to scatter toys

the woman sometimes wished for a small
cramped space she did not have to own,
though that would be the same as wishing
that the boys—now three of them—would

shrink into the immaterial
past where the woman is still
free to sit in temporary rooms
and brood, her body hollow and un-

belonged. And in the silence of boys
at school the woman sits in the hollow
of her deeded house, its immense weight
settled now into foundation,

the hairline fissures of adjustment
now plaster-mended. She never owned
this house, just as she cannot keep
her boys from passing through its rooms

with wakes of scattered junk and pieces
of babyhood and boyhood they treasure
and forget (though never quite cast
aside, which means the woman must).

She sorts and stores and gives away
and is wearied by the objects of
the too physical world
left for her to tend. But in

the mornings when the baby's cry
stirs the house into migration,
boys padding to the parents' bed
and burrowing between—limbs

crisscrossed so no body is
itself alone—then the silence
of slow awaking seems supported
by the pressure-treated, nail-gunned

beams of renovation, that nest
of taxes, bills, and warranties
which blow away now in the clean,
scrubbed clerestory light designed

to fall across our faces, so that
we rise, become our separate but
connected selves, leave the house
its empty ticking noises, measured lot.

—*Suzanne Matson*

Walls

Our old single-wide trailer, walls thin as an alibi on Monday morning. Cracked wood veneer and hollow pocket doors filter nothing: not the steel screams as my brother twists guitar strings into Frankenstein sutures, not his friend Bob's head on the linoleum floor in the hallway like distant artillery—*thump, thump, thump, thump*; he wants to crack his skull open, release something distant. I hear my mother's litanies about the price of gas and hamburger, school clothes or electricity whisper in my ears, or the hiss of match to dry tobacco in hand-rolled cigarettes late at night as she studies at the kitchen table. Outside, the guttural engine tearing up our driveway under pre-dawn stars, buckshot scatter of gravel. Then, my father's eruption, dreadful jingle of his keys, boots staggering across the floor, curses like razorblades slashing portals to the underworld. In the morning, dogs scramble outside, their ritual barking a race with the sun; *whoosh* as our propane stove flares, battered coffee pot a tin clank on grate. Black: no sugar, no milk, no cream. Birds' feet skitter across the sheet metal roof; the language of wings. Hard rain makes a drum of our home's thin skin. Brown beer bottles clatter into paper bags. My mother's silence louder than my ears can bear. Her sharp glance tells me to listen, not speak. I am good at it. I am careful, obedient, all ears and no tongue – until the day I put pencil to paper like a key to a lock, and a never-ending story falls out into the surprised world. But where else did they expect that cacophony to go?

—*Deborah A. Miranda*

Divorce Is an Aquarium Not a Boat

The house counts keys   seals shut the fire draft
but the banister sharpens   its balustrade for shins

and family-room curtains   collaborate with moon—
let chilled silver leak   through turncoat glass

swab sills and floors   with liquid anesthetic
that numbs the wings   of the creased leather chair

where father used to read   fairy tales to boy and girl
while mother took up needles   to knit and purl the night

casting even blue wool   in almost-perfect loops.
They floated together   in a boat of yellow light.

Tonight they snap the lights   and negotiate the stairs
to unravel their vows   divided under down

ignorant of moon   that soaks the red rug
licks Legos from the stool   drowns the Dr. Seuss.

Gaunt clock hands   time the icy tide
that inundates the kitchen   laps carpet on the stair

extinguishes the hall-light   shaped like a shell.
The mother and the father   dissolve in dreams.

The children suck whimpers   from wet pink thumbs
rock in whitewater   wicking the chill.

At the foot of the stairs   in the cold tank of light
a shape starts to move—   a sickle-tail, a fin.

Something like a shark   noses broken toys,
hunts up the humming   aquarium of moon.

—*Judith H. Montgomery*

If the Glass House Be the Woman's

Let it be glass brick, the kind art-deco builders mortised
into bath and bedroom windows--

some ridged and furrowed like corduroy,
some bumpy like clouds--they'd allow light

but not seeing in. The slate roofs, opaque,
would blind the higher powers,

the hawks, gods, and crop dusters.
If you look out, the wooded ridges sky

touches, the redbud bleeding out,
and even Marge's zinnias next door,

a fiesta that maddens the bees,
are washes, beautifully imprecise,

Muir watercolors.
The mail man's uniform

blue, duller than Klee's or sky's,
comes and goes, a vertical cloud.

Looking in, he sees only smear
and blur, but you are seeing

unseen, emperor of the eye,
hiding in a house of light,

the glass's smear and erasure
your asylum, your immunity.

—*Mary B. Moore*

House Angels

Smoke circles the roof like a dark halo.
Inside the house a fire rages. When I enter
        a man is sitting down to dinner.

The people who live here, I ask, where are they?
I am about to eat them, he says, won't you join
        me? They are so delicious when fresh

and I have plenty. I couldn't, I say,
I am too fond of those people.
        No, no, these are not your people, he says.

They're mine. Please try one.
They look like my pajamas you're wearing, I say.
        And isn't that my coffee mug?

He shrugs his shoulders and digs in,
placing a napkin on his lap.
        I leave the house I thought

was mine and wander through the neighborhood
that is less and less familiar,
        intruding on men who consume their families,

looking for the right house with the right people,
where the children I left on the fire
        are more than ready.

—Peter E. Murphy

Trouble's Voice

It's the quiet again that's shaken me
   up from the night's deepest dream,
      where the old row house rocked me

and sang like a freight car, like a refugee
   grandmother, into this blank hour
      of not a birdcall, no freeway drone, no

intimate's snore, not a wind in its shifting
   factions among the trees, no whit
      of a whispered argument—nothing

of what, as I grew, I found I could
   drift to, the night's giants stomping
      and swearing downstairs, the day's

cocksure gods sniping and spitting
   over me while knees on carpet I leaned
      at my next gang-lord mansion of cards.

The music that soothed me was gripe
   and seethe, tongues whipping across
      the table at crowded feasts, bang

and clatter of angry kitchens—floating
   in that sweet-and-sour din, I grew
      like a circus kid who knew how to not

let the air go still. We'd fill in the merest
   starts of silence with splashy refrains,
      flash a display over each new abyss,

trained in exchanging abrasions. Stings
   at the surface would do. Call someone
      a name. Slap a cheek. There's relief

in such sudden hurt—it tips a heart
    back out of the grief-chasm. Now,
        in this dark's sheer lack of disturbance

no peace—I listen for trouble's voice.
    Grant me, at least, a good grunted curse
        in the hall. Then maybe I'll sleep.

—Jed Myers

It Seems Like a Room

It seems like the familiar
light upon the familiar body.
It seems like a room in which the mirror is a door
that lets pass only what you think you are.
A room comfortable in its colors, simple
in its purpose. It seems like your room,
like the room you share,
the room you dream of. It seems
like the room you return to when the world
has had its way. A room with the expected
things: curtains, carpet, the sense
of suspended time. It seems like a room
rich with all you've enjoyed, memory
in the fabrics, memory in the wood.
A room in all ways possible, except
that it is not a room. It is not
moonlight rendering it to your eyes.
It is not daylight nor dusk nor fluorescence,
not a room in candlelight.
It is not a lover's body rocking above yours,
not a lover's voice saying,
This, here—know it and remember.
It is not a room but it seems like one.
Yet you rise to touch it,
the traffic of faces in the mirror.
It seems like your face, this one before you now.
It seems like the face you've given everything for.

—*Christopher Nelson*

The Doghouse

When Mom told Dad he was still in the doghouse,
I didn't know what that meant, especially
since Ray--short for Stray, Dad said--had a nice house
that Mom and I picked out. He stayed in there a lot,

resting his head on his paws, watching the grass
grow, Dad said, not a care in the world. Sometimes
while he sniffed around the yard I'd crawl into Ray's
house and look out at mine pretending I didn't know

who lived there. I liked the big pot of flowers beside
the back door, and I tried to see inside the windows
but they were too bright and far away. Ray always
came running and licked my face until I got out.

How I learned what it meant to be in the doghouse
I don't know. But whenever I hear the expression
I think of my Dad. And Mom. And Ray and the house
where I grew up knowing I was loved. And nothing else.

—*Eric Nelson*

Mother of Roses

and clematis that vined the trellis near the pond
 and crepe myrtles that flared across the field

  where the barn leaned, hesitating
 before the inevitable fall, rest now.

The choices have all been made. On the porch,
 where hummingbirds whirred at the red feeder,

  I waited for your verdict: *I'll take the rocker*
 or I'll need the smaller of the two dressers.

What I dreaded: *I'm staying here after all.*
 Instead, you shrank in your chair like a child

  waiting for punishment, saying nothing.
 When I was ten, and you might or might not

have even noticed, the neighborhood kids and I
 would haul out quilts, lay them over limbs,

  clothespin them into doorways, rooms.
 Sometimes, one of us would die—the mouth

fallen open, head rolled to the side,
 eyes fixed, just like on *Rawhide.*

  It never occurred to any of us to consider
 the deceased's wishes for disposition of the body.

We waited for the sudden intake of air,
 jumped up and played some new game.

  In the bedroom, where you slept one week
 on one side of the bed, one week on the other,

while the movers arrived with their dollies and boxes
       and the blue walls bore the light from the window,

you lamented: *I was happier in this house*
       than anywhere else I have ever lived,

then escaped to that half-lit corner
       of your basement. I pointed to the loveseat,

          the bedside table, the microwave, only
what would fit in the new place.

The new owners built a stable. The pond
       dried up in drought, refilled in plentiful rain.

          The barn finally fell, Queen Anne's lace
burgeoning among the tangled, twisted timbers.

—*Kathy Nelson*

Your Little House

—*i.m. Doug, a good neighbor (1946–2015)*

The little houses on our street
fall one by one
to fashion or decay,
whatever moves the world along.
The week you left,
another house came down.

We told the stories
that its walls contained
as we watched the backhoe slam
through brick and pane,
peeling memory back,
parlor, kitchen, bath,
until it finally unveiled
the most intimate of spaces.
A life-sized dollhouse
into whose rooms
we placed each vanished
woman, child, and man.
With one wild swing,
the wrecker's arm rammed
the roof and last supporting wall.
The small house caved
like a pricked balloon,
its noisy ruin a hail of grit
that sent us running
and took it back to earth.

You knew the frailty
of mortar, brick and wood,
yet understood what's market value,
what's true worth. Whatever
love and skill can do,

you said, our little houses
will not last. Foundations crumble,
shingles crack; seals blow
and let the cold wind pass.

Even so, you
fixed what you could
until all fixing failed.

—*Suzanne Nussey*

Nuthatch Lane

The house will go soon to someone
who may not know it needs its gutters
cleaned in autumn, the fescue cut in June
before it grows thigh-high. Someone new
will rake a million pine needles twice every
summer, thousands of pinecones, roll
them, load after load, to the burn pile out
back. Someone new will open the windows
wide in mid-July, set the fan on high, scurry
the mice from the garage, spiders from
the closets, from under the beds. We'll leave
our memories in the corners, beneath
the stairs, places where dust collects—
an errant gray hair, flakes of skin rubbed
into the slatted floor or spun invisibly into
a web slung from the vaulted ceiling.
It's not that bad—leaving—a freedom,
we tell ourselves. We'll still be happy, have
the moon, each other, for some number
of years. There'll be days when the drift
of pine scent will find us, the staccato beat
of the red-tailed flicker tap-tap-tapping.

—*Hari Parisi*

Breaking Home

A broken house
housebroken by the weight
of boredom, waiting. Look
into the bore domed in its stones,
a window pane. The pain winnowed
through mortar around the door,
which stands mortified, ajar.
In the kitchen, a jar lid
stares upward. Upstairs, tears
in the wallpaper look like tears
shed from lids too full to hold.
Out back, a shed rendered useless
surrenders to the soil. Used less,
would it be so moldered, so dark?
In darkness, mold twines lines
that grout through grout-lines,
the white marble sink now mottled
and marred like the motley wood-work,
mismatched and sinking, working along
the floor. A beveled wood stove, matches
scattered, a cracked basement floor:
the sunken level. Cement cracks as steel beams
strain to level an egress that steals sunbeams,
represses light like the light fixture,
never fixed, suspended in the master
bedroom. In the end, who masters whom
if there is no room? A garden bed, a driveway.
All regarded too quickly and while driving away.

—*Tory V. Pearman*

A Dependency

You can lose your brother to Hell
and still be happy inside your house.
The house has many rooms. You find
elegance in its brown walls and furnishings,
and though the flames that rush past
the window make everything bright inside
with the dozens of doors closed,
you can streak all over and no one
will ever see you. If you had neighbors,
you'd bring out your brown china and crystal,
and bourbon you'd pair with browned
hors-d'oeuvres. You'd invite them
over to see your view of the fires
even as they're envious enough to break in.
You don't get used to the heat, but you were
born in a hot place, so you tell yourself
you're suited to rising temperatures.
You never understood the white sheets
of the bedrooms, why your brother
had opted to sleep. It takes hours,
but you manage to fall asleep, being
so still that your dreams take you away
to a mountaintop, a world of greens
and violent and churning blues. In
your house in Hell, there's a nightstand,
a white picket fence around a porch.
You meet a girl, a brown lamp
with a brown shade, and every moment
of happiness in the house with your eyes open
is one you realize your brother is missing.

—Dustin Pearson

At the Foster Home

—for my mother

The food you just ate is a simple nothing,
its name and taste swallowed by a ravenous mouth
not your own. You say the meal was fine,
"just fine," then minutes later ask me
when you're going to finally get
something to eat.
                The easiest to remember,
I am the one you fear has forgotten you—
my daily visits gone minutes after
I kiss you goodbye. Each day you ask me
where I'm going. Every day you ask me to please
explain where you're staying. You tell me again
you're being "a good girl"—ashamed when you
can't remember where the bathroom is, stunned
then subdued to see your bedroom set, clothes,
and family portraits appear from behind
an unfamiliar door. You accept with only a wince
your belongings shrunk to what a single room
in a stranger's house can hold.
                      Yours isn't even
a casting away—no knitting needles, bridge decks,
or driver's license knowingly laid to one side,
then to be remembered and mourned. The victim
who wanders in shock through a ransacked life,
you stare at vacant spots, unable
to even guess
          what once was there.

—Paulann Petersen

The House Teaches Her about Love

They seemed a stream of need flowing by her legs,
five or six of them, seven, she wasn't sure, children,

young, vague, but the house would help her
keep them alive. It was large and light—

                here, we're safe, she sighed,

meaning absence, mainly, from vigilance,
the mind twisting, cat-eared, to clicks and creaks,

snap-deciding now again now
about which sounds not to fear.

She ran to secure each window and door,
all locked, all tight.

                    Except that one.

Fumbling with the latch
she saw outside a darkness outlined in dark—

and now she had to get them out out, quick,
away from the house that, dammit, wasn't hers anyway

just shelter she'd found by chance, and those kids
weren't hers either, you know.

               —*Susan Azar Porterfield*

Zu Hause / At Home

Until I started kindergarten,
my lullaby—*a Nachtlied*,

Mama singing of *Sternlein*—
little stars, instead of twinkle,

twinkle—English I didn't know
I didn't know. In 1960s Detroit,

the streets—Dresden, Westphalia,
the stores—*Gerhardt's Delikatessen*,

Hermann's Backerei, our table
set for *Kaffee* and *Kuchen*,

for couples I called *Onkel, Tante*,
who talked like my parents did,

of *kein Pfennig!*—not a penny!—pockets
empty when they'd boarded ships,

sailed across *der Ozean*. Deutschland
was a map in my storybook—

Brüder Grimm, was a place Papa
and Mama penned letters to,

Familie on both sides of Berlin.
At Christmastime, on birthdays—

sighs of *Heimweh*—that hurt for home
I pictured like a bandaged sore,

and always, tales of war, of running
through streets, farm fields, woods—

Bomben dropping from the sky,
history burning at my feet.

—*Christine Rhein*

A House Called Tomorrow

You are not fifteen, or twelve, or seventeen—
You are a hundred wild centuries

And fifteen, bringing with you
In every breath and in every step

Everyone who has come before you,
All the yous that you have been,

The mothers of your mother,
The fathers of your father.

If someone in your family tree was trouble,
A hundred were not:

The bad do not win—not finally,
No matter how loud they are.

We simply would not be here
If that were so.

You are made, fundamentally, from the good.
With this knowledge, you never march alone.

You are the breaking news of the century.
You are the good who has come forward

Through it all, even if so many days
Feel otherwise. But think:

When you as a child learned to speak,
It's not that you didn't know words—

It's that, from the centuries, you knew so many,
And it's hard to choose the words that will be your own.

From those centuries we human beings bring with us
The simple solutions and songs,

The river bridges and star charts and song harmonies
All in service to a simple idea:

Is ourselves. And that's all we need
To start. That's everything we require to keep going.

Look back only for as long as you must,
Then go forward into the history you will make.

Be good, then better. Write books. Cure disease.
Make us proud. Make yourself proud

And those who came before you? When you hear thunder,
Hear it as their applause.

—*Alberto Rios*

Empty

The carpet, the walls, refrigerator, closets,
all cleaned, empty as they were before
he moved in, no trace of his predecessor
whose daughter surely stood at the threshold

as I do now, key in hand to return
to the Transition Counselor who is sorry
for my loss and is on her way up
to make sure I've removed all personal

belongings, which I've already sorted through:
sweaters I gave him still wrapped in tissue paper
arms folded across chests, while all he wore
was an old beige cardigan, coffee-stained

and thin at the elbows. So much he never used:
rolls of toilet paper, a bottle of gin,
three decks of cards still sealed in plastic.
$21.00 in a brown leather billfold.

I'm staring at four divots in the carpet
where the table stood until I had it carted out,
the table he'd owned for 70 years that he,
son of a furniture salesman, recognized

for its quality wood and at which he sat
each morning eating breakfast. When we first
looked at the apartment, the woman showing
us around extolled its nondescript shades.

Everything neutral so nothing would clash,
his old life would segue into this new one
which, we all knew but didn't say,
would be the last one that he would live.

—*Susan Rothbard*

A Pool of Tears

*"I wish I hadn't cried so much!' said Alice, as she swam about,
trying to find her way out. 'I shall be punished for it now, I
suppose, by being drowned in my own tears!"*
—Alice in Wonderland, *Lewis Carroll*

Only a very small wrong, I thought, unraveling
the bobbins in mother's sewing basket, but the threads
were pretty spread across the floor, and in all this
awful rain the colors so cheerful.

After my scolding I must have cried myself to sleep
and now wade down the stairs, hungry for a snack
but wonder if I may be still in my bed, only dreaming
that water is filling my shoes, rising to my knees,

soaking my skirts with each step down into the foyer.
But I must be awake for the water is so cold and mucky,
and I'm shivering, calling for mother. Has she floated
away? Surely she would not leave without me!

I'm swept into the parlor where all sorts of odd things
float about—a stew pot and pictures and chairs, and now
down the hallway the upright comes thumping a water-
logged moan, followed by the bench spilling sheet music.

Oh, it's all too dreadful! It seems my tears have flooded
the house and now the water is rising clear to my chin.
I must keep treading, but my arms are so tired.
Here's a chair leg I'll hold on to 'til father comes home.

But how will he ever get in? And now a swell
has carried me through to the pantry
where rhubarb and oranges go bobbing; maybe
our house has tumbled into the sea—

if I could just reach the biscuit tin, I might grow bigger
and see my feet again. Look! There's the shore and a dodo,
holding out my thimble in his strange bird hand, and
beside him Mother with her sewing basket, beckoning.

—*Barbara Sabol*

How to Move In

Bring in the bed first.
Then the books.
Then wait as long as possible before doing anything else.

Go back to work. Sweep out the old place.
Volunteer.
Allow time for your books to adjust their spines

in light of a different dust sifting the air
and the low deep notes sounded by floor joists when
no one's there.

Let the books and the light in the room
settle in.
Let the bed be.

Because the promise of sex
is almost as good as sex and sometimes better, let's face it,
so let the bed rest.

The world remains packed
with injustice, cockroaches, pottery shards
and improbable physics,
all none of your choosing

so allow emptiness
to work its little acre
in your life.

Then you'll be home.

—*Hayden Saunier*

Central Ave.

Along the avenue a regiment of trees
stood rigid, and in the house as big as a
Saturday the clocks ticked on amid stagnant air,
slack doorknobs, paint chips—

the rumble of casings and pocket doors.
Such images culled from memory
travel in a slow migration
of thought, clogging the throat with things.

From the old garage that clung to the flanks of the house
like a lesser organ to the girl who dragged a bicycle
out by its neck, past the grease pit, ice pick, wood beams
and the grass that waited for no one.

Inside the basement's underground life
remained calm: ash box, vice grip, hook
and eye; reliable occupants
biding their time.

It is not the memory of wood
to be blamed, or the dining room's
hermetic servitude where dust motes floated
like lost chromosomes.

The house and the girl kept their distance
from the adult figures who idled
in dim lit rooms, meal after meal,
words masticated like tough meat.

Perhaps their story still remains
staged among the accoutrements of desire;

Playboys, stockings, cologne, a bed
too wide to fill. Memory, as usual speaks

in the sudden recollection of rooms.
Small wonder the girl left
for homes less perilous
and the avenue was endless.

—*Tina Schumann*

Elegy for the Long Dead

Once there was a girl
with a full trunk
of lace and beeswax

given to a man
with forty acres, a rough-
beamed house on a hill.

She perfected the art
of biscuits, cooked her hens'
eggs in cast iron.

How warm it always was,
and in the quiet night,
she waited

for him to slowly pull
the ribbons of her bodice,
to take her breast in his hand.

Now theirs is one of those
homesteads seen from the highway,
disappeared

to just a set of flagstone stairs
in a field, leading nowhere.

In what were rooms, yarrow
and snake grass. The barn
choked with kudzu.

But there is something
in the way a dragonfly wants
a pane to tap its wings against.

Her blackberries still grow
along the thorny fence,
giving their blossoms to bees.

This couple has a thousand
grandchildren who will never
find their way home.

To their descendents, they are just names
and dates on the first page
of a cracked-spine Bible.

—*Danielle Sellers*

Deep in Milkweed

My grandfather shuffled
his family to a few

sloping acres he'd wrangled
in the country, a crudely

framed shack—shallow
footings, foundation,

studs, flimsy roof.
No insulation

or running water, a single
wood stove, old

sheets for bedroom walls.
He'd thought to finish

the house by fall, collapsed
into pneumonia, lost

his job. Winter crept in.
His sons lined

the tarpaper shell with newsprint.
They slept in mittens,

coats over sweaters, three
to a mattress. Between

coughs, he swore he'd plumb
the place, put up

drywall when spring swept away
the ice. In the warm

seasons, he prayed each
day for easy

breath, died before the parched
leaves dropped.

His children, angular and thin,
rambled the hill

deep in milkweed. Sharp
pods scraped

their skin as they scanned for monarchs.
Tufts of floss

released, ribboned the empty
heat, the sky.

—*Annette Sisson*

Ash

Strange house we must keep and fill.
House that eats and pleads and kills.
House on legs. House on fire. House infested
With desire. Haunted house. Lonely house.
House of trick and suck and shrug.
Give-it-to-me house. I-need-you-baby house.
House whose rooms are pooled with blood.
House with hands. House of guilt. House
That other houses built. House of lies
And pride and bone. House afraid to be alone.
House like an engine that churns and stalls.
House with skin and hair for walls.
House the seasons singe and douse.
House that believes it is not a house.

—*Tracy K. Smith*

Foxes

Displaced—they scavenge, circle
the house, drive the dog wild,
cry themselves hoarse for a mate.

Down the road the ground's
cleared: blue shadow &
white relief, a stubble of broken

growth, wood scraps & ripped
greenery: a torn line of trees.
Houses are going up.

Foxes are on the move.
The pond dries in July,
peepers pitch a racket

from the rushes and tall weeds.
A neighbor keeps a shotgun
propped against the screen door.

For sport, he fires pellets
at carpenter bees nesting in
hay bailed in the back field.

But at night the foxes have him
worried: they circle the house,
avoid the razed lot, scream:

the sound of a murdered woman—
streaks of copper in a blue
and bleached-bone night.

—Kyla Sterling

Acclimatize

The passive house—the home my husband
and I watched from skeleton
of board and steel to walls thick
with insulation, the house our son
thinks is ours because he kicked up
sawdust running along its planks—
features a homogenous
interior temperature,
sustainable despite winter's
negative forty-degree days.

In our skin's cells, intrinsic
heat works from a brush of a hand,
an ode to staircase, or a photo
of a well-worn dwelling. And when sundogs
appear, they glitter against the gauze
of sunrise, and I recall the morning
my husband arrived with snow frozen
in his hair, icicled eyelashes melting
from my touch. He helps build for balance;

our son, however, is a creature
of the cold. On nights the wind chill vacuums
breath, our preschooler spins stories
of ice railroads and woolly mammoths.
Yet after a full day of sledding
and sipping on snow-cones, he slipped into
our bed, between us, for warmth. He's
the reason I know that cold shifts
DNA. Relationship or
house—we design for heat.

—*Christine Stewart-Nuñez*

The Cabbage

You have rented an apartment.
You come to this enclosure with physical relief,
your heavy body climbing the stairs in the dark,
the hall bulb burned out, the landlord
of Greek extraction and possibly a fatalist.
In the apartment leaning against one wall,
your daughter's painting of a large frilled cabbage
against a dark sky with pinpoints of stars.
The eager vegetable, opening itself
as if to eat the air, or speak in cabbage
language of the meanings within meanings;
while the points of stars hide their massive
violence in the dark upper half of the painting.
You can live with this.

—*Ruth Stone*

Self-Portrait as Homestead

You take a good look   something
you've been avoiding all these years
your skin a kind of peach stucco
the hallway blurred

with clutter. You glue and staple
each shingle   each summer   add
magenta   cerise   apple   your mother's
anger   your father's storm

drains and floorboards   his tongue
and groove. His silence. You patch
Catholic prayers   gilt
wallpaper and beach sand

add undressed
windows   your hysterectomy
scar. A good house is a used place
turned over and passed on

a place of winter noons
layered like the cemetery
with strange names.
You're still holding everything—

skin cells and your grandmother's
cookbook   broken outlets
and not enough income.
You wanted a light-filled house

with wood floors and unexpected
rooms. A possible place   the way
womb hums the sound of *home*.
What you got were too-small

closets and this hard squint
appraising what you thought you needed
all of it catalogued here   in this edifice
of doors and stories and bones.

—*Jeri Theriault*

The Empty House

House that we bought just a month before
we were married; after the wedding, the rooms
unfolded anew. House where I brought

the baby straight from the hospital, sat
at the dining room table, unbuttoned my blouse.
House of the Christmas Eve dinners,

my niece and her boyfriend together
on the piano bench, which to this day
bears a mark from the heat of their thighs.

House of the homework assignments, the three of us
up half the night making two-inch-tall tepees
of bark from the birch tree and little plaid bedrolls

cut from an old flannel shirt. House
so toxic with anger, a teenager's
venomous mouth, that for three years

we dared not have anyone over for dinner.
Then, when she left us for college,
a silence so vast

we inflicted our surplus endearments
on a long-suffering 12-year-old cat.
House of near-human sounds—

bone-creaks and moaning, sighing and wailing
in storms. House of our long years of marriage,
your limbs entwined around mine

like ivy around the round stones
of the stone walls surrounding the yard.
House of the woodpile, the woodshed,

the canvas wood carrier carried
six times a day from the shed
to the wood stove, the smell of felled maple

and oak. House I came home to after
my mother died, put down
my suitcase and lay on the bed

with my coat still on, hands
folded over the knot of my sorrow
as sleep closed its massive green door.

—*Sue Ellen Thompson*

Copulations

The woman from the zoo said a bird often sneaks copulations

with the next-door neighbor bird

while her male is off getting nesting material.

A man I know collects milligrams

of potassium, ugly yams and containers

of coconut water, near obsession

when basic staples are needed for the pantry. Another gathers

nothing, his body so flagrant with indifference

who can blame mother bird?

I've sought my neighbor

for ham sandwiches, conversation,

her male off accumulating knowledge

and roughage when all she wants is her name

bouncing about his mouth. I will tell my son

when he's older to keep it simple—

bright throws for a home's sofa,

scraps of paper for handwritten messages,

maybe farm honey and a grooved

wooden dipper. My grandfather often arrived with an earnest

purchase: egg cups in pairs for his collection, each small

round emptiness anticipating the planet's most perfect food.

He brought home songs with moons doing things,

sang refrains about give and take

while my grandmother happily flapped

her rugs against the porch door to his birdsong.

—*Marjorie Thomsen*

Old Snow

My Michigan irises—dug up
by Mom and Dad after they sold their house
but before they moved, brought along

in grocery sacks of dirt when they drove out
to visit, then replanted in my yard—

are blooming in New Jersey. "It's strange,"
Mom says, "to buy a house and think
it's probably the last one we'll ever buy."

Of ten sisters and brothers, she's the oldest
of the seven still alive. We're talking

long-distance, Kingston to Lansing, and I close
my eyes to picture her sitting in the kitchen
with her coffee. In the in-between quiet

I hear the plink-plunk of April rain
on the stone path outside my kitchen,

the brief jangle of wind chimes
tangling in the wind. Part of me thinks I could
live here forever, part of me can't wait

to pack it all in. Though in this pandemic
spring (and soon summer, then fall, winter

and spring) we stay home: the backyard's
my narrow kingdom. I sit on the patio, lucky
to have a job, lucky I can do it on a laptop,

lucky to hear Chuck Wilkens in the next yard,
explaining to co-workers in Germany

how he makes sun tea, and then Adelaide
on the other side, practicing her cello.
I can't name the composer, but know

the melody when she plays it, plays it again
and again all morning—teasing out that

complicated knot near the end. It feels like
this strange way of living won't end
but each day is a gift: Yesterday

on FaceTime, Mom asked, "How're
those irises doing?" and I held the phone

so she could see. They help her remember
and still, each spring, they surprise me:
inky purple, off-white like old snow.

                    —*Matthew Thorburn*

Another Blue

—after "Small Blue Town" by Maggie Smith

There is a small blue house
living inside me—blue chimney,
blue doors, blue windows,
blue floors, blue shadows under
the bowl of peonies on the blue
piano—an exact replica of the place
where I was born. Blue pines,
a pool of blue shade beneath
their blue branches, blue barn,
blue fields, blue of chicory blooming
beside the blue road, puffs of dust
blue beneath bare feet. Blue thread
of Perkiomen Creek running
at the bottom of the hill, blue
bridge built by the WPA stretching
across it. Blue scent of water
in the air, blue of dew in the mint
beneath the arbor where blue grapes
grow. Blue of hayfields rolling
away at dusk, blue of bob-whites calling.
Blue of home, a ridge of the Appalachians
visible in the blue distance, beyond
the wide blue sill piled with books.
Blue of forever, blue of gone. Blue
of a girl in a nightgown with blue flowers,
reading a blue book, as I write
blue words on a page divided
into blue lines, each one a blue highway
stretching between then and now.

—Alison Townsend

Heart by Heart the House

will empty, thread by thread all hems

unstitch.

Not even the twin oaks will last, though their roots

insist themselves,

buckling the limestone

drive. Tonight you fly,

above your head, our arthritic cat who has lived

too long to protest, who will probably be the next

to go. I am trying

not to cling. I am trying

to remember the look

flooding your father's face that

morning he discovered tomatoes destroyed

despite his careful fencing. What could he do

but plant again

in the furnace of a new day's heat, thinking

of your mother cooking, that very minute, corn

gleaned yesterday from his garden? Maybe

we'll bring into this world five children and ruin

     every one, regardless of inoculations, safety belts,

  Tot-Finder decals silver

in their windows—that may serve no purpose

    but to remind them to be afraid of fire, my own

  childhood fear—flames

  raking the irreplaceable—with me still

but disappearing. Sometimes—even

    as cell by cell we're breaking, even

    as my mind, more sieve than cup, lets go of you, lets go—I

    am overtaken by a moment's calm, relieved

     not to know what's coming. Do I want us

  to die at the same time and turn

  into trees or start over

as ourselves: our first

  encounter, kiss, our great mistakes

    ahead

  —Rhett Iseman Trull

House Dreaming

Twice I drove by my old house during Covid
to see if it had adapted to its latest owners.

Was this now their nest for future dreaming,
for finding places to hide and remember spaces?

Sometimes I dream about our other house without
an attic but with a labyrinth for a basement,

rooms for playing dress up, the loud furnace
room. The workshop and closet of bottles,

the house urban renewal tore down. A house
wraps itself around you. You can still go there

and its walls hold you up even when the rooms
are gone. The place you live keeps the rain out,

keeps the sun off your skin, but offers its windows
to watch the sun set where your cousin

is gathering up dolls whose hair she bobbed.
After you leave a house, you can still see

where your mother buttered toast or where you kept
the bread on the refrigerator so the cat wouldn't

eat holes in the bag. In the pantry, you can see
the applesauce on the shelf with the extra bottle

of ketchup, the knives lined up perpendicular
in their drawer. You can see the morning glories,

the way cooks look out windows as they stir batter
to be sure the dog hasn't jumped the fence. You can

see the yellow sponge in the bathtub, your brush
on the sink. You can see the way light slants through

the basement window near the furnace's glow when it kicks on,
in harmony with all irrationality of depths and empty space.

—*Maryfrances Wagner*

The Barn

The barn came with the house. It needed work.
        The strength of her sons to shore up the beams.

Summer settled like haze then emptied
        all at once, left a place for goldenrod so soon

that she was wholly unprepared
        for the seasons in between. Now the state

of being caught between two places
        is familiar. She mistakes the seasons

and the faces, recollects the names,
        keeps the quilts in vacant guest rooms

while today is wintering down.
        This found art of making everywhere

a haven is her task, time an overflowing
        cup that's spilling reason, memories ajar

like barn doors wide on broken hinges,
        hay-heavy odor soaking air, starlings

rising—they gust over the barn on strings
        pulled by the wind, her thoughts adrift, the loft

now roofless, its summer view distant, emptied.

—*Elinor Ann Walker*

To the Buyer of Our Old Home

We can tell you, if you want, which doors creak,
   or windows that need to be re-glazed, which faucet
has a tendency to leak, and where a wine glass
   left a halo etched in the counter's travertine.
And we could share which walls absorb sadness,
   till morning light leans in comforting the contours
of the bed, but chances are you'll learn this
   on your own. There's the cough of the AC kicking on,
and the hiss of the heater turning off, and a crack
   in the plaster by the stairs. You'll study it at times
as metaphor, disaster creeping like the bifurcated lines
   of your palm. But then again, maybe you won't....
Let's go outside.

The doorbell never works when it rains. And the riot
   of white gardenias blooming now is always late.
A black snake burrows through ferns, and a cardinal
   spends days hurling himself against our bare window.
We say *our*, but it's your house now. Our beloved dog
   was buried over there—along with his chew toys
and bones. And at night our kids' laughter carries
   through the courtyard of the home (though they
moved out some years ago). And this large oak—
   what can we say? Old limbs keep falling even when no
wind stirs. The tree is gone. We sold because we couldn't
   chop it down. Still, we hear the woodpecker crazed
as the leaves turn brown.

—Helen Wallace

Brooklyn Walk-Up

Too often my mother told the story

Of bundling me into the red snowsuit,

Leaving me scarved & ear-flapped,

Zippered to the chin, baby-bootied

Upon the quilted bed

While she wrestled the carriage

Six flights down tenement steps

Only to return to a locked door,

The key nestled in the handbag

Dangling from the inside hook.

A cry like no other rose inside her.

She rushed again down crooked stairs

Out onto Covert Street,

Past the deli & funeral parlor,

All the way around the corner

To the Irving Avenue alley

Where she grasped then climbed—

This new mother—

The fire escape ladder

Rung by icy rung

To reach the first metal landing, then

Clanged upward floor by floor until,

Crouched upon the uppermost grate,

She could see the swollen,

Immobile, doll-shaped pile.

She raised the unclasped window,

Gathered me, grabbed her bag, descended

Once more the six floors to the cold carriage,

Then raced to the Dekalb Avenue BMT

To meet my father home from work.

Wheeled madly, I slept like a bobbing cork.

She never told him how she'd shut me in,

How she'd gazed through glass

At the clump of cloth,

The breathing heap of wool & cotton

For which she'd leapt beyond her measure.

Motherhood had turned uncommon.

Years later she took such pleasure

In repeating the story, that boy

Swathed like an Andean child

Sacrificed on the mountain peak,

Mummified by the dry, glacial winds,

Never to name his executioner,

That boy her favorite version of me.

—*Michael Waters*

House of Giants

Imagine constructing your home
of behemoth bones, like the homes
found in Ukraine's Dniepr River valley
from as long ago as 23,000 BCE.
Each one made from hundreds
of mammoth bones and tusks,
covered with hides for warmth,
centered around a hearth.
Imagine the power vested in you
by these giants as you sit, safe
and warm, carving with stone tools
while your children play.
Imagine being able to imagine
in that firelight, a future where
your clever descendants invent
the written word. Invent trauma care.
Invent megacorps. Invent war.
What might you say to them
from your magnificent shelter,
its ceiling arched with ribs?

—*Laura Grace Weldon*

Leaving the House

Nights, nights, and these dreams of houses accumulate.
Clapboard, shingle, stucco, brick, these houses are mine
but I never can stay in them. Wounded, they are, or sick.

And for a while I take care of them. Are they grateful?
They point their fingers, they chase me away. And just
when I think it's over and done, another house dream

comes along. How many years does this go on? It's true:
the house we live in right now is a nice house, a good house.
This house has a view of the city, back yard and trees,

its own personality thanks to paint and new furniture finally
come to some kind of truce with mine. But does calling a truce
erase grief? And you, who thought we should move from the one

I adored, who knew better than I about loans and financial
advantage, not even you could stop me from doing crazy things.
Fantasized taking a lover. Stopped writing. Told our daughter

one day after school that her birthday bunnies had been killed
overnight by raccoons, told her right in front of a group of kids
at her brand-new school, who saw her crying and from that day

laughed in her face. What could I have been thinking?
Who knows? And who knows this: can ever a house refuse
to be home? That old house we bought for a song and moved

across town like a soul rescued from drowning, held all my
vows of forever. Abandoned, abandoned, shining as childhood,
all that lavish promise, every well-rubbed floorboard and sill.

—*Ingrid Wendt*

Invasive Species

I moved Manhattan aside with my hands
I moved its chessboard of avenues and streets
moved from a metropolis
to less ocean, more trees
                            Around me I placed a stone house
There I moved the species that didn't belong
with my hands
                I cut them once
then let them grow again, cut them down
to the roots and drowned them
                            There, I moved the invasio
into my body, swallowing
phragmites, flowering
rushes, Japanese sedge and Cypress Surge, their beauty
bittersweet and milk toxic, I swallowed
                            slender cotton snake
even yellow daffodils even red iris
because they too didn't belong

This morning, across the opening
of our driveway, a deer
                    dead less than an hour
his furred antlers loose
his body still warm

I moved the car, rented a van
moved from a city to acres of black oak and beech
                            but I don't belong
any more than the barberry and buckthorn
My strangeness as unsalvageable
                        as the herd
                        on the other side of this wall
that will, at a single sound, run full tilt
into oncoming headlights
Their terror is both key and the keyhole

I am not fit to be either
I choke on the deer, the willow
and the white dogwoods shadowing him
I try to be quiet when moving

—*Sarah Wetzel*

Bearing Wall

A crack runs vertical—*uh oh*.
My wife inclines one cautionary brow.
White pine floorboards bow downhill,
slow sedimental flow
beneath foundation stones. Last line
against collapse this wall
resists encroaching gravity and time
with honeycombs of lath, plaster
cladding over beams and columns
braced by hand. *Good bones*,
the broker offers hopefully,
white lie to gild the obvious.

I see again the curtained bed
we stood around, stoic but adrift.
Our mother lay half-conscious,
flush with metastatic cancer,
every bone a hive the CAT scan
mapped like valleys of the moon.
She'd fallen hard, a broken thigh;
we couldn't bear to tell her this was it.
Unaware, *just dropping by*,
the orthopedist planned to operate.
My brother cursed and left the room.

Now I trace another fracture
floor to ceiling, back again,
feel years of weight
compressed behind, immense—
a family's inheritance—
push out. *We'll let you know*,
I say, and like that surgeon's face
the broker's sags, admitting false
pretense: what's ruined cannot stay
or be repaired, it's gone,

a knockdown, total loss,
as when she stirred awake and groaned,
I'm done with this
and everything gave way.

—*George Witte*

House

In the house of be-quiet-and-sleep

In the house of no apples and sharpened knives

In the house where your father would not come to live

    if your mother died

    or your mother, your father

In the house of fat bees falling into the wine

    swatted mid-swoon

    in their lust for flowers

In the house of cut flowers, cut green

    at their throats and stripped

    of their petals, breath by breath

In the house like a narrow box tilted askew

    in which we were shaken like broken toys

In the house of the dull of our lord the unkind

In the house of shut-up and lock-the-doors

    and only one door to the world, one to sky

—Cecilia Woloch

A Vocabulary of Home

On weekends my parents took me along to open houses,
mansions with winding halls, hidden alcoves, secret stairwells,
and multiple kitchens. We wandered through imagined lives
where pantries were shelved with canned beans and bottled jams,
breads and teas, tiers of jarred food ordered to the ceiling,
like ledged cliffsides lifting bushes from a thread of roots
that snaked through cracks in the rock. We entertained
a fantasy of histories in the banisters and landings,
a presence pausing in its wet boots and wool sweater
to recall the warmth of one who could make these empty rooms
cozy, the narrative of other lives older than ours finding light
in antique splendor. I nestled into remote corners
shadowed in a depth of discrete wonder, a privacy as vast
as a valley with a window seat. I climbed to the highest levels
where an attic bedroom pitched cavernous walls and a turret.
From that circle of windows streets stitched the outskirts of town
to wheat fields dotted with red and rusting tractors, sparrows
spiraled through the golden spears and up, lacing sunlight
into a tapestry, first words of a story so intricate, and colored
with such nuance, I stepped into its road lined with trees
and joined my song to the birds in their crowns.

—*Michael T. Young*

Small House Breathing

Awakened by a storm at midnight
I listen for it while my eyes slide down walls
with reflected rivulets of Cape Cod rain.
Lightning flashes like thoughts
of a child come to me. The ticking
I hear is that of my watch and then, only when
I place it on my ear. Last night, a friend's
newborn yelped into the phone as
she told me of her wonder at this
new universe of two. The night is wild
with creation. An insomniac Nature
tosses in her bed, too restless to let me sleep.
Another flash of lightning and I see my
lover as a boy running the streets of Beirut, snipers
poised in their nests, thunder of shelling. My mother
and father sleep on the other side of the wall.
I hear their breathing between gusts of rain.
I hear the small house breathing, its walls
running with water, air filled with the smell of salt,
the house itself become a womb.

—Claire Zoghb

Contributors

Susan Aizenberg is the author of *A Walk with Frank O'Hara: Poems* (University of New Mexico Press, 2024.) She is also the author of two earlier full-length collections, *Quiet City* (BkMk, 2015) and *Muse* (Crab Orchard, 2002), and co-editor with Erin Belieu of *The Extraordinary Tide: New Poetry by American Women* (Columbia University Press, 2001). She is Professor Emerita at Creighton University and lives in Iowa.

Nin Andrews is the author of 15 poetry collections, most recently *Son or a Bird: A Memoir in Prose Poems* (Etruscan Press, 2025). She is also the recipient of two Ohio individual artist grants, the Pearl Chapbook prize, the Wick Chapbook prize, the Gerald Cable Award, and the Ohiona Award for Poetry in 2016. Her poetry has been translated into Turkish, performed in Prague, and anthologized in England, Australia, and Mongolia.

Cheryl Baldi is the author of *The Shapelessness of Water* and *Cormorants at Dusk*. A former Bucks County Poet Laureate, she was a finalist for the Frances Locke Memorial Poetry Award and a 2023 Pushcart Prize nominee. She divides her time between coastal New Jersey and Bucks County, Pennsylvania, where she volunteers for the Poet Laureate Program and the Arts and Cultural Council.

Tony Barnstone teaches at Whittier College and is the author of 23 books, most recently *Apocryphal Poems* (Nirala Press, 2024). He is also the author of *Faces Hidden in the Dust: Selected Ghazals of Ghalib* and *The Radiant Tarot: Pathway to Creativity*. Among his awards are the Poets Prize, Pushcart Prize in Poetry, John Ciardi Prize, and fellowships from the NEA, NEH, and California Arts Council.

Stuart Bartow (1951–2024) was a much beloved professor at SUNY Adirondack, as well as one of the founders of the Battenkill Conservancy, which he chaired for several decades. He was the author of many books of lyric poetry as well as collections of haiku, lyrical essays, and haibun. His final collection, *The Whole Shebang: New and Selected Poems*, was published by The Word Works in 2025.

Joseph Bathanti is the former North Carolina Poet Laureate (2012–14) and the recipient of the North Carolina Award in Literature, the state's highest civilian honor. The author of over 20 books, he is the McFarlane Family Distinguished Professor of Interdisciplinary Education at Appalachian State University. He was inducted into the North Carolina Literary Hall of Fame in October of 2024.

Michele Battiste is the author of several books, including *Waiting for the Wreck to Burn*, which won the Louise Bogan Award from Trio House Press, and *The Elsewhere Oracle* from Black Lawrence Press. She works for a global conservation nonprofit raising money to tackle climate change and protect biodiversity. She also teaches workshops.

Jan Beatty's eighth book, *Dragstripping*, was published by the University of Pittsburgh Press in 2024. Her memoir, *American Bastard*, won the Red Hen Nonfiction Award. Her other books include *The Body Wars* and *Jackknife: New and Selected Poems*, which won the Paterson Poetry Prize. She is Professor Emerita at Carlow University, where she directed creative writing, Madwomen in the Attic workshops, and the MFA program.

Jeanne Marie Beaumont is the author of five collections of poetry, most recently *Lessons with Scissors* (Tiger Bark Press, 2024). Her verse play, *Asylum Song*, had its premiere production at HERE Arts in New York in the spring of 2019. She has taught at Rutgers University, the Stonecoast MFA Program, and the 92nd Street Y.

Regina Berg is an emerging black poet from Chicago now residing in Pflugerville, Texas. Her work has been published in *BarBar, The Bluebird Word, Pictura Journal,* and *Sybil.*

George Bilgere is the author of eight poetry books, most recently *Central Air* (University of Pittsburgh Press, 2022). He has received grants and awards from the Pushcart Foundation, the Fulbright Foundation, the NEA, the Witter Bynner Foundation, and the Ohio Arts Council. He teaches at John Carroll University in Cleveland and hosts a weekly poetry radio program called *Wordplay.*

Michelle Bitting is the author of six poetry collections, including *Nightmares & Miracles* (Two Sylvias Press, 2022), winner of the Wilder Prize and named Best of Indie 2022 by Kirkus Reviews. Her chapbook, *Dummy Ventriloquist*, was published in 2024. Her poetry has been featured on *The Slowdown* and published in such journals as *Thrush, Cleaver*, and *The Missouri Review.*

Sally Bliumis-Dunn is the author of three full-length books, most recently *Echolocation* (Plume Editions, 2018). She is Associate Editor-at-Large for *Plume Poetry.* Her poems have appeared in *New Ohio Review, The Paris Review*, and *Prairie Schooner* and have been featured on *The Writer's Almanac, Poem-a-Day*, and *American Life in Poetry.*

Jody Bolz is the author of three books of poetry: *A Lesson in Narrative Time* (Gihon Books), *Shadow Play*, and *The Near and Far* (both from Turning Point Books). Her poems have appeared in such journals as *Ploughshares, Prairie Schooner*, and *Poetry East.* Executive editor of *Poet Lore* from 2002–2019, she now serves as poetry editor for *Moment Magazine.*

Laure-Anne Bosselaar is the author of *The Hour Between Dog and Wolf* and *Small Gods of Grief*, winner of the Isabella Gardner Prize. Her fourth collection, *These Many Rooms*, was published by Four

Way Books. *Lately*, her new and selected, came out from Sungold Press in 2024. Recipient of a Pushcart Prize and the James Dickey Poetry Prize, she served as Santa Barbara's Poet Laureate from 2019–2021.

Rebecca Brock is the author of *The Way Land Breaks* (Sheila-Na-Gig Editions, 2023). Her work appears in *The Threepenny Review, Thrush, Whale Road Review*, and elsewhere. In 2022, she won the Woman's Poetry Prize from Kelsay Books. She lives in Virginia with her family. She has been a flight attendant for most of her adult life and is still surprised by this fact.

Theresa Burns is the author of the poetry collection, *Design* (Terrapin Books, 2022), and the chapbook, *Two Train Town* (Finishing Line Press, 2017). Her writing has appeared in *The New York Times, Prairie Schooner,* and *New Ohio Review*, and has been featured on *Verse Daily*. Winner of the 2023 New Jersey Poet's Prize, she is director of Watershed Literary Events and teaches writing in and around New York.

Elena Karina Byrne served as a final judge for PEN's "Best of the West" award, the Kate and Kingsley Tufts Poetry Awards, and the international Laurel Prize. Her five poetry collections include *If This Makes You Nervous* (Omnidawn). Her poetry and non-fiction have appeared in *Poetry, Best American Poetry, The Pushcart Prize* anthology, *American Poetry Review, Poem-a-Day*, and elsewhere.

Robin Rosen Chang is a 2023 New Jersey State Council on the Arts Poetry Fellow and the author of the full-length collection *The Curator's Notes* (Terrapin Books, 2021). Her poems have appeared in *Alaska Quarterly Review, New Ohio Review,* and *Plume*, and have been featured on *Verse Daily*. She has an MFA from the Program for Writers at Warren Wilson College and teaches writing at Montclair State University.

Patricia Clark is the author of *O Lucky Day* (Madville Publishing, 2025), *Self-Portrait with a Million Dollars* (Terrapin Books, 2020), and three chapbooks. She has work in *Plume, The Southern Review, North American Review*, and elsewhere. Her poem "Astronomy: 'In Perfect Silence'" was chosen to go to the moon as part of the Lunar Codex on a NASA Space X flight in fall 2024. She lives in Michigan.

Billy Collins served two terms as the US Poet Laureate from 2001–2003. He also served as the New York State Poet Laureate from 2004–2006. He has received fellowships from the NEA, Guggenheim Foundation, and New York Foundation for the Arts. He is the author of 13 books of poetry, most recently *Water, Water* (Random House, 2024).

Ginny Lowe Connors is the author of six poetry collections, most recently *White Sail at Midnight* (The Poetry Box, 2024). Her chapbook, *Under the Porch*, won the Sunken Garden Poetry Prize. She holds an MFA in poetry from Vermont College of Fine Arts and runs a small poetry press, Grayson Books. A Board Member of the Connecticut Poetry Society, she is managing editor of *Connecticut River Review*.

Beth Copeland is the author of *Shibori Blue: Thirty-six Views of the Peak* (Redhawk Publications, 2024). Her earlier books include *Blue Honey*, the 2017 Dogfish Head Poetry Prize winner, and *Traveling Through Glass*, the 1999 Bright Hill Press Poetry Book Award winner. She has been profiled as poet of the week on the PBS NewsHour website. She lives in the Blue Ridge Mountains of North Carolina.

Jim Daniels' fiction book, *The Luck of the Fall*, was published by Michigan State University Press in 2023. Recent poetry collections include *The Human Engine at Dawn* (Wolfson Press, 2022), *Gun/Shy* (Wayne State University Press, 2021), and *Comment Card* (Carnegie Mellon University Press, 2024). He lives in Pittsburgh.

Christina Daub is both a Pushcart Prize and Best of the Net nominated poet whose work can be found in several anthologies and literary journals, including *Connecticut Review, The Cortland Review, Poet Lore*, and *Potomac Review,* among others. Her work has been translated into German, Italian, and Russian. She co-founded *The Plum Review*.

Heather L. Davis earned a BA in English from Hollins University and an MA in creative writing from Syracuse University. She is the author of *The Lost Tribe of Us*, which won the 2007 Main Street Rag Poetry Book Award, and has published poems, short stories, and essays in journals, such as *Quartet, Gargoyle*, and *Poet Lore*. She lives in Pennsylvania.

Jessica de Koninck is the author of *Cutting Room* (Terrapin Books, 2016) and the chapbook *Repairs* (Finishing Line Press). Her poems have been featured on *The Writer's Almanac* and *Verse Daily* and published in *Valparaiso Poetry Review, Paterson Literary Review, diode*, and elsewhere. She co-edits ALTE, a multi-platform publication, and lives in New Jersey.

Claire Denson's writing appears in *The Cincinnati Review, The Missouri Review,* and *The Iowa Review,* among other journals. She has received support and awards from Brooklyn Poets, Martha's Vineyard Institute of Creative Writing, the University of Michigan, and the University of North Carolina at Greensboro, where she earned her MFA. She is a Teaching Artist at the National Book Foundation in NYC.

Theodore Deppe is the author of eight collections, most recently *Impossible Blackbird* (Arlen House, 2024). He has received a Pushcart Prize and two NEA fellowships. He worked as a nurse for twenty years, then taught in MFA programs in Ireland, the UK, and the US. Since 2000, he has lived in Ireland.

Natalie Diaz is the author of *Postcolonial Love Poem* (Graywolf Press, 2020), winner of the Pulitzer Prize in Poetry. She is also the author of *When My Brother Was an Aztec* (Copper Canyon Press, 2012), winner of an American Book Award. Her honors include fellowships from the Lannan Literary Foundation, Native Arts Council Foundation, and Princeton University, as well as the 2023 Arts and Letters Award in Literature.

Stuart Dischell is the author of six poetry collections, most recently *The Lookout Man* (University of Chicago Press, 2022). His poems have appeared in the *Best American Poetry* anthology and the *Pushcart Prize* anthology. A recipient of awards from the National Poetry Series, NEA, North Carolina Arts Council, and Guggenheim Foundation, he teaches in the MFA Program at the University of North Carolina Greensboro.

Kelly DuMar is the author of four poetry collections, including *jinx and heavenly calling* (Lily Poetry Review, 2023). Her poems have been published in *Bellevue Literary Review, Tupelo Quarterly, Thrush,* and elsewhere. Her images have been featured on the cover of such journals as *About Place, Josephine Quarterly,* and *Synkroniciti.* She teaches creative writing workshops and lives in Boston.

Lisken Van Pelt Dus teaches poetry, languages, and martial arts in Massachusetts. Her work can be found in such journals as *Naugatuck River Review, Third Wednesday Magazine,* and *Sky Island Review.* Her books include *What We're Made Of* (Cherry Grove, 2016), *Letters to My Dead* (Three Bunny Farm, 2022), and *How Many Hands to Home* (Mayapple Press, 2025).

Dina Elenbogen is the author of the poetry collections *Shore* and *Apples of the Earth,* and the memoir *Drawn from Water.* Her work has appeared in such journals as *Lit Hub, Bellevue Literary Review,* and *Prairie Schooner.* She has an MFA in poetry from the Iowa Writers' Workshop and teaches creative writing at the University of Chicago Writer's Studio.

Rebecca Ellis has published poems in *About Place Journal, American Journal of Poetry, Bellevue Literary Review, Beloit Poetry Journal,* and elsewhere. She edited Cherry Pie Press, publishing poetry chapbooks by Midwestern women poets. She is a Master Naturalist through the University of Illinois Extension Service and lives in southern Illinois.

Robert Fillman is the author of *The Melting Point* (Broadstone Books, 2025), *House Bird* (Terrapin Books, 2022), and the chapbook, *November Weather Spell* (Main Street Rag, 2019). His poems have appeared in such journals as *Salamander, Spoon River Poetry Review,* and *Tar River Poetry.* He teaches at Kutztown University.

Annie Finch is the author of seven volumes of poetry, including *Calendars* and *Eve* (Story Line, 1997), both finalists for the National Poetry Series, and *Spells: New and Selected Poems* (Wesleyan University Press). Her other books include *A Poet's Craft* and ten anthologies. Based in New York City, she travels the world to teach and perform.

Ann Fisher-Wirth's eighth book, *Into the Chalice of Your Thoughts*, is a poetry/photography collaboration with Wilfried Raussert. Her seventh book is *Paradise Is Jagged* (Terrapin Books, 2023). She coedited *Attached to the Living World: A New Ecopoetry Anthology* (Trinity University Press, 2025). A senior fellow of the Black Earth Institute, she received the 2023 Governor's Award in Poetry from the Mississippi Arts Commission.

Alice B. Fogel was New Hampshire's Poet Laureate 2104–2019. Her seven poetry collections include *Falsework, Nothing But, A Doubtful House*, and *Interval: Poems Based on Bach's "Goldberg Variations."* Recipient of an NEA fellowship, she is also the author of *Strange Terrain*, a guide to appreciating poetry. She works one-on-one with neurodiverse students at Landmark College.

Rebecca Foust's poems won the James Dickey Prize and the Fischer Cantor Prize in 2024, and the New Ohio Review Prize in 2023, and have appeared in *Poetry, Ploughshares*, and *The Southern Review*. She is the author of eight poetry books, most recently *Only* (Four Way Books, 2022), and a chapbook, *You Are Leaving the American Sector* (Backbone, 2024).

Jennifer L Freed's *When Light Shifts: A Memoir in Poems* was a finalist for the Sheila Margaret Motton Prize. Her work has appeared in *Atlanta Review, B O D Y, Rust and Moth*, and elsewhere. Her awards include the Frank O'Hara prize and the Samuel Washington Allen Prize. She teaches adult education programs in Massachusetts.

Alice Friman's eighth collection of poems is *On the Overnight Train: New and Selected* from LSU Press. Her earlier book, *Vinculum*, won the Georgia Author of the Year in poetry. She has received three prizes from The Poetry Society of America, two Pushcart Prizes, and inclusion in *Best American Poetry*. Her work has been published in *Poetry, Ploughshares, Plume*, and elsewhere.

Timothy Geiger is the author of four full-length poetry collections, most recently *In a Field of Hallowed Be* (Terrapin Books, 2024), and ten chapbooks. His honors include a Pushcart Prize; a Holt, Rinehart, and Winston Award in Literature, and the Vern Rutsala Poetry Prize. Proprietor of Aureole Press, a letter-press imprint producing chapbooks of contemporary poetry at the University of Toledo, he lives in Ohio.

Maria Mazziotti Gillan is the Founder and Executive Director of the Poetry Center at Passaic County Community College in Paterson, New Jersey. She is also the Editor of the *Paterson Literary Review* and Professor Emerita of English and creative writing at Binghamton

University-SUNY. Her newest poetry collection is *When the Stars Were Still Visible* (Stephen F. Austin University Press, 2021).

Susana Gonzales has lived in 24 homes. Growing up on Air Force bases resulted in a strong need for home and much of her poetry explores that necessity. She has been published in various anthologies and journals, including *The Power of the Feminine I, Sheila-Na-Gig, One Art,* and *As You Were: The Military Review.*

Jessica Goodfellow's poetry books are *Whiteout* (University of Alaska Press, 2017), *Mendeleev's Mandala,* and *The Insomniac's Weather Report.* A former writer-in-residence at Denali National Park and Preserve, she has had poems in *The Southern Review, Ploughshares, Scientific American,* and *Best American Poetry.* She lives in Japan.

David Graham's most recent book is *The Honey of Earth* (Terrapin Books, 2019). He also co-edited *Local News: Poetry About Small Towns* and the essay anthology *After Confession: Poetry as Autobiography.* Individual poems, essays, and reviews have appeared in journals and anthologies as well as online. He retired from college teaching in 2016 and now lives on the edge of the Adirondacks.

Benjamin S. Grossberg's books of poetry include *My Husband Would* (University of Tampa, 2020), winner of the 2021 Connecticut Book Award, and *Sweet Core Orchard* (University of Tampa, 2009), winner of a Lambda Literary Award. He also wrote the novel, *The Spring before Obergefell,* winner of the 2023 AWP Award Series James Alan McPherson Prize. He is Director of Creative Writing at the University of Hartford.

Barbara Hamby has published seven books of poems, most recently *Burn* (2025), *Holoholo* (2021), and *Bird Odyssey* (2018), all from the University of Pittsburgh Press. Her poems have recently appeared in *The New Yorker, American Poetry Review, Ploughshares,* and *Sixth Finch.* She teaches at Florida State University where she is a Distinguished University Scholar.

Jeffrey Harrison is the author of seven books of poetry, most recently *Between Lakes* (Four Way Books, 2020) and *Into Daylight* (Tupelo Press, 2014), winner of the Dorset Prize. His honors include fellowships from the Guggenheim Foundation, the NEA, the Bogliasco Foundation, and multiple appearances in both *Best American Poetry* and the *Pushcart Prize* volumes.

Leslie Harrison's third book, *Reck* (Akron), came out in 2023. Her second book, *The Book of Endings* (Akron), was a finalist for the National Book Award. Her first book, *Displacement,* won the Bakeless prize in poetry from the Bread Loaf Writers' Conference and was published in 2009 by Mariner Books, a division of Houghton Mifflin Harcourt. She divides her time between Baltimore and the Berkshires.

Donna Hilbert's latest book is *Enormous Blue Umbrella* (Moon Tide Press, 2025). Her work has appeared in numerous journals and broadcasts including *Rattle, Sheila-Na-Gig,* and *One Art,* and has been featured in *Vox Populi, The Writer's Almanac,* and *Lyric Life.* Her work has also been included in such anthologies as *The Poetry of Presence, The Path to Kindness,* and *The Wonder of Small Things.*

Cindy Ellen Hill is the author of *Wild Earth* (Antrim Press, 2021), *Elegy for the Trees* (Kelsay Books, 2022), *Mosaic: Poems and Essays from Travels in Italy* (Wild Dog Press, 2024), and *Love in a Time of Climate Change* (Finishing Line Press, 2025). Her poetry has been included in *Treehouse Literary Review, Flint Hills Review, Anacapa Review,* and *The Lyric.*

Andrea Hollander's sixth full-length poetry collection is *And Now, Nowhere But Here* (Terrapin, 2023). She is the winner of two Pushcart Prizes (poetry and literary nonfiction) and two poetry fellowships from the NEA. In 2011, after more than three decades in the Arkansas Ozarks, she moved to Portland, Oregon, where she created The Ambassador Writing Seminars, which she taught in her home until the pandemic and now via Zoom.

Amorak Huey is the author of four books of poems, including *Dad Jokes from Late in the Patriarchy* (Sundress, 2021). He is co-founder of River River Books and co-author of the textbook *Poetry: A Writer's Guide and Anthology* (Bloomsbury, 2024). Recipient of a fellowship from the NEA, his poems have appeared in *Best American Poetry, The Southern Review,* and *Poem-a-Day.* He teaches at Bowling Green State University.

Saba Husain is the author of the poetry collection *Elegy for My Tongue* (Terrapin Books, 2023). Her work has appeared in *Barrow Street, Cimarron Review, On the Seawall,* and *Third Coast,* and has been featured on *Verse Daily.* She serves on the board of Mutabilis Press and lives in Texas.

Alison Jarvis's work has appeared in such journals as *Gulf Coast, New Ohio Review,* and *The Seattle Review.* She is a recipient of the Guy Owen Prize, The Mudfish Poetry Prize, the Lyric Poetry Prize from the Poetry Society of America, and a fellowship from the MacDowell Colony. Her collection, *Where Is North,* received the Gerald Cable Award. She is a psychotherapist in private practice in Brooklyn.

Jeffrey N. Johnson's fiction and poetry have appeared in *The Sewanee Review, Birmingham Poetry Review, South Dakota Review,* and the *Southern Poetry Anthology.* His story collection, *Other Fine Gifts,* won a Mid-Atlantic regional Ippy Award, and his novel, *The Hunger Artist,* was a finalist for the Library of Virginia's People's Choice Award.

Lois P. Jones' first poetry collection, *Night Ladder,* was a finalist for the Julie Suk Award. She won the 2023 Alpine Fellowship in poetry as well as the Bristol Poetry Prize. Her work has been published by the Academy of American Poets, *Image, Poetry Wales, Plume,* and elsewhere. She is the poetry editor of the Pushcart prize-winning *Kyoto Journal.*

Tina Kelley's *Rise Wildly* appeared in 2020 from CavanKerry Press, joining *Abloom & Awry, Precise,* and *The Gospel of Galore,* a Washington State Book Award winner. She reported for *The New York Times,* has written two nonfiction books, and is the recipient of a 2023 Fellowship Finalist award from the New Jersey State Council on the Arts.

Adele Kenny has been a Paterson Poetry Prize finalist and the recipient of poetry fellowships from the New Jersey State Council on the Arts, a first place Allen Ginsberg Poetry Award, and Kean University's Distinguished Alumni Award. Founding director of the Carriage House Poetry Series and poetry editor of *Tiferet Journal,* she has twice been a featured reader at the Geraldine R. Dodge Poetry Festival.

Jane Kenyon (1947–1995) was the author of *Constance* (1993), *Let Evening Come* (1990), *The Boat of Quiet Hours* (1986), and *From Room to Room* (1978). She was married to the poet Donald Hall and lived with him at Eagle Pond Farm, Hall's ancestral home in New Hampshire. At the time of her death from leukemia, she was New Hampshire's Poet Laureate.

Lynne Knight is the author of six full-length poetry collections, most recently *The Language of Forgetting* (Sixteen Rivers Press, 2018) and *The Persistence of Longing* (Terrapin Books, 2016). She is also the author of six chapbooks. Recipient of a Rattle Poetry Prize and an NEA fellowship, she lives on Vancouver Island.

Ted Kooser is the author of thirteen collections of poetry, including *Raft* (Copper Canyon Press, 2024) and *Kindest Regards: New and Selected Poems* (Copper Canyon Press, 2018). His awards include two NEA fellowships in poetry and the Stanley Kunitz Memorial Prize. He served as the thirteenth United States Poet Laureate from 2004 to 2006. He lives in rural Nebraska.

Judy Kronenfeld's sixth full-length book of poetry is *If Only There Were Stations of the Air* (Sheila-Na-Gig, 2024) and her third chapbook is *Oh Memory, You Unlocked Cabinet of Amazements* (Bamboo Dart, 2024). Her poems have appeared in such journals as *New Ohio Review, One Art,* and *Rattle.*

Susanna Lang is the author of three collections of poetry, most recently *Travel Notes from the River Styx* (Terrapin Books, 2017). She was the 2024 winner of the Marvin Bell Memorial Poetry Prize from *December Magazine.* Her work has appeared in such publications as *Tupelo Quarterly, American Life in Poetry, Rhino Reviews,* and *The Slowdown.* She divides her time between Chicago and Uzès, France.

Hailey Leithauser's books are *Swoop* (Graywolf, 2013), winner of the Poetry Foundation's Emily Dickinson First Book Award and the Towson Award for Literature, and *Saint Worm* (Able Muse Press, 2019). Her work has appeared in journals and anthologies including *Agni, The Gettysburg Review, Poetry*, and *The Crafty Poet: A Portable Workshop*, and has been selected four times for the *Best American Poetry* series.

Svetlana Litvinchuk is the author of a debut poetry chapbook, *Only a Season* (Bottlecap Features, 2024). Her poetry has appeared in *About Place, Plant-Human Quarterly, One Art, Apple Valley Review*, and elsewhere. She is the reviews editor for *Only Poems*. Originally from Kyiv, Ukraine, she now lives in Missouri.

Eric Lochridge is the author of *My Breath Floats Away from Me* (FutureCycle Press, 2022). He is pursuing an MFA in the Rainier Writing Workshop and serves as an associate poetry editor for *Okay Donkey* magazine. His poems appear in *Diagram, Slipstream, Whale Road Review, Psaltery and Lyre*, and other literary journals.

Marjorie Maddox has published 17 collections of poetry, including *Transplant, Transport, Transubstantiation; Begin with a Question*; and *Seeing Things*. She was also co-editor of the anthologies *Common Wealth: Contemporary Poets on Pennsylvania* and *Keystone Poetry*. Professor Emerita of English at Commonwealth University, she is *Presence* assistant editor and WPSU-FM *Poetry Moment* host.

Jennifer Maier works as a professor and Poet-in-Residence at Seattle Pacific University. Her work has received the 2012 Emily Dickinson Award and two Visiting Artist Residencies from the American Academy in Rome. Her books include *Dark Alphabet* (Southern Illinois University Press, 2006), *Now, Now*, and *The Occupant* (both from University of Pittsburgh Press, 2025).

Suzanne Matson is the author of two volumes of poetry, *Sea Level* and *Durable Goods*, and four novels. Her poems have appeared in *American Poetry Review, Poetry, Shenandoah*, and elsewhere. Her fiction has appeared in *The Harvard Review, Carolina Quarterly*, and as a *Ploughshares Solo*. She teaches at Boston College.

Deborah A. Miranda is the author of the hybrid project, *Bad Indians: A Tribal Memoir*, which won the PEN Oakland Josephine Miles Literary Award. She is also the author of four poetry collections, including *Indian Cartography*, as well as co-editor of the Lambda finalist *Sovereign Erotics: An Anthology of Two-Spirit Literature*. She lives in Oregon.

Judith H. Montgomery's chapbook, *Passion*, received the Oregon Book Award for Poetry. Her second full-length collection, *Litany for Wound and Bloom*, a finalist for the Marsh Hawk Prize, appeared in 2018. Her prize-winning narrative medicine chapbook, *Mercy*, appeared from Wolf

Ridge Press in 2019. Her most recent chapbook, *The Ferry Keeper*, received the 2024 Grayson Books Chapbook Competition prize.

Mary B. Moore's sixth poetry collection, *Amanda Chimera*, the Arthur Smith Poetry Prize winner, appeared in 2025 from Madville Publishing. Her previous collection, *Dear If*, was a finalist at Orison Books in 2022. She is also the author of two prize-winning chapbooks, *Amanda and the Man Soul* and *Eating the Light*. She lives in West Virginia.

Peter E. Murphy is the author of a dozen books and chapbooks of poetry and prose, including *A Tipsy Fairy Tale: A Coming of Age Memoir of Alcohol and Redemption* about growing up in Wales and New York City. The founder of Murphy Writing of Stockton University in Atlantic City, he leads writing workshops in the US and Europe.

Jed Myers is the author of three books of poetry, most recently *Learning to Hold* (Wandering Aengus Press, Editors' Award, 2024), and previously *The Marriage of Space and Time* (MoonPath Press) and *Watching the Perseids* (Sacramento Poetry Center Book Award). His poems have appeared in *Prairie Schooner, Rattle, Poetry Northwest,* and elsewhere. He lives in Seattle, where he is editor of the journal *Bracken*.

Christopher Nelson is the author of *Blood Aria* (University of Wisconsin Press, 2009) and five chapbooks, including *Blue House,* winner of a Poetry Society of America Fellowship. The recipient of the 2023–24 Amy Lowell Traveling Scholarship, he is the founding editor of Green Linden Press.

Eric Nelson has published seven collections of poetry. His most recent, *Horse Not Zebra*, was published in 2022 by Terrapin Books. His previous books include *Terrestrials*, chosen by Maxine Kumin for the X.J. Kennedy Award; *The Interpretation of Waking Life*, winner of the University of Arkansas Poetry Award; and *Some Wonder*, which won the Gival Press Poetry Award. He lives in North Carolina.

Kathy Nelson is the author of *The Ledger of Mistakes* (Terrapin Books, 2023). She is a James Dickey Prize winner, an MFA graduate of the Warren Wilson Program for Writers, and a Nevada Arts Council Fellow. Her work has appeared in *Five Points, New Ohio Review, Tar River Poetry,* and elsewhere. Her work has also been featured on *Verse Daily*. She lives in Nevada.

Suzanne Nussey is the author of *Slow Walk Home* (Saint Julian Press). She is an MA graduate of Syracuse University's creative writing program. Her poetry, creative non-fiction, and essays have appeared in Canadian and US magazines, anthologies, and online publications. Working as a freelance writer and editor in the areas of religion, psychology, and health and wellness, she has facilitated writing workshops for unhoused women.

Hari Parisi's (formerly Hari Bhajan Khalsa) poems have been published in numerous journals, most recently in *Atlas and Alice, Paper Dragon,* and *Poetry South*. She is the author of three collections of poetry, including *She Speaks to the Birds at Night While They Sleep*, winner of the 2020 Tebot Bach Clockwise Chapbook Contest. She has recently returned from the city to her hometown in the heart of Oregon.

Tory V. Pearman resides with her family in Ohio, where she teaches literature and writing. Her work appears in journals such as *Westchester Review, Salamander, Atticus Review,* and *San Pedro River Review*. Her work has been nominated for the Pushcart Prize and the Best of the Net.

Dustin Pearson is the author of *A Season in Hell with Rimbaud* (BOA Editions, 2022), *A Family Is a House* (C&R Press, 2019), and *Millennial Roost* (C&R Press, 2018). He is an assistant professor in the Department of English Language and Literature at the University of Toledo.

Paulann Petersen, Oregon Poet Laureate Emerita, has eight full-length books of poems, most recently *My Kindred* from Salmon Poetry of Ireland. Her poems have hitched rides on buses and light rail cars in Oregon and Washington. Because the Latvian choral composer Eriks Esenvalds has used her work as lyrics for his compositions, her poems are being sung by a number of university and church choirs.

Susan Azar Porterfield is the author of four books of poetry, most recently *Voice/Poems* (Trio House, 2025). Previous books include *In the Garden of Our Spines, Kibbe* (both from Mayapple Press), and *Dirt, Root, Silk,* which won the Cider Press Review Editor's Prize.

Christine Rhein is the author of *Wild Flight*, a winner of the Walt McDonald Book Prize (Texas Tech University Press, 2008). Her poems have appeared in journals, including *The Southern Review, Michigan Quarterly Review*, and *Rattle*, and in anthologies, including *Best New Poets* and *The Best American Nonrequired Reading*. A former automotive engineer, she lives in Michigan.

Alberto Rios served as the inaugural Poet Laureate of Arizona, 2013–2015. He is the author of sixteen books of poetry and prose, most recently *Every Sound Is Not a Wolf* (Copper Canyon Press, 2025). He is the recipient of the Arizona Governor's Arts Award, six Pushcart Prizes, the Walt Whitman Award, and fellowships from the Guggenheim Foundation and the NEA.

Susan Rothbard is the author of *Birds of New Jersey*, which won the 2020 Dogfish Head Poetry Prize and was published by Broadkill River Press. Her poetry has appeared in *The Cortland Review, Paterson Literary Review, Poet Lore,* and *Southern Poetry Review*, among other journals. Her work has also been featured in Ted Kooser's *American Life in Poetry* and *Verse Daily*.

Barbara Sabol's most recent book is *Watermark: Poems of the Great Johnstown Flood of 1889* (Alternating Current Press, 2023.) Her collection, *Imagine a Town*, won the 2019 contest from Sheila-Na-Gig Editions. She received an Individual Excellence Award from the Ohio Arts Council and was named the Arts Alive 2024 Literary Artist. She lives in Ohio.

Hayden Saunier is the author of six poetry collections, most recently *Wheel* (Terrapin Books, 2024). Her work has been awarded a Pushcart Prize, the Rattle Poetry Prize, and the Pablo Neruda Prize. Her work has also been published in such journals as *Beloit Poetry Journal, diode, Plume,* and *VQR,* and has been featured on *Poetry Daily, Verse Daily,* and *The Writer's Almanac.*

Tina Schumann is the author of four collections of poetry, most recently *Boneyard Heresies* (Moon City Press, 2024). She is editor of the anthology *Two-Countries: U.S. Daughters and Sons of Immigrant Parents* (Red Hen, 2017). Her work has been published in such journals as *Cimarron Review, The Missouri Review,* and *Rattle,* and has been featured on *Poetry Daily, Verse Daily,* and *The Writer's Almanac.*

Danielle Sellers is the author of *Bone Key Elegies* (Main Street Rag, 2009) and *The Minor Territories* (Sundress Publications, 2018). Her poems have appeared in *Prairie Schooner, The Cimarron Review, Poet Lore,* and elsewhere. She teaches Literature and Creative Writing at Trinity Valley School in Texas.

Betsy Sholl served as Poet Laureate of Maine from 2006 to 2011. Her tenth collection of poetry, *As If a Song Could Save You* (University of Wisconsin Press, 2022), won the Four Lakes Prize. Her ninth collection, *House of Sparrows: New and Selected Poems,* was published in 2019. She teaches in the MFA in Writing Program of Vermont College of Fine Arts.

Annette Sisson is the author of two full-length collections of poems, most recently *Winter Sharp with Apples* (Terrapin Books, 2024). Her poems have appeared in *Birmingham Poetry Review, Rust & Moth, Cumberland River Review,* and elsewhere. Her awards include The Porch Writer Collective's 2019 poetry prize. She teaches at Belmont University and lives in Nashville.

Tracy K. Smith served as the 22nd Poet Laureate of the United States from 2017–19. She is the author of five poetry collections, including *Such Color: New and Selected Poems,* winner of the 2022 New England Book Award; *Wade in the Water,* winner of the 2018 Anisfield-Wolf Book Award; and *Life on Mars,* recipient of the 2012 Pulitzer Prize. Recipient of a 2024 Guggenheim Fellowship, she teaches at Harvard University.

Kyla Sterling earned her MFA in poetry at UNC-Greensboro. Her work has appeared in *Adroit Journal, Blackbird, Painted Bride Quarterly, Radar Poetry, Barrow Street Journal,* and *Notre Dame Review,* among others. Her first chapbook, *Warnings & Fables,* was published by Dancing Girl Press. She lives in Georgia.

Christine Stewart-Nuñez served as South Dakota's Poet Laureate from 2019–2021. She is the author of three poetry collections, most recently *The Poet & The Architect* (Terrapin Books, 2021). Her collection, *Bluewords Greening* (Terrapin Books, 2016), won the 2018 Whirling Prize. She currently teaches at the University of Manitoba in Winnipeg.

Ruth Stone (1915–2011) was the author of 13 books of poetry, including *Ordinary Words* (1999) which won the National Book Critics Circle Award; *In the Next Galaxy* (2002), winner of the National Book Award; and *What Love Comes To: New & Selected Poems* (2008), a finalist for the Pulitzer Prize. Her awards included two Guggenheim Fellowships, the Bess Hokin Prize, the Wallace Stevens Award, the Shelley Memorial Award, and the Walter Cerf Award for Lifetime Achievement in the Arts.

Jeri Theriault is the author of *Self-Portrait as Homestead* (Deerbrook Editions, 2023). Her awards include the 2023 Maine Arts Commission Literary Arts Fellowship, the 2023 Monson Arts Fellowship, and the 2022 NORward Prize from *New Ohio Review*. Her work has appeared in *The Rumpus, The Asheville Review, Plume,* and elsewhere. She lives in Maine.

Sue Ellen Thompson is the author of six books, most recently *Sea Nettles: New & Selected Poems.* She has won a Pushcart Prize, the Pablo Neruda/Nimrod Hardman Award, two individual artist grants from the State of Connecticut, and the 2010 Maryland Author Award from the Maryland Library Association. She teaches at The Writer's Center in Washington, D.C.

Marjorie Thomsen teaches others how to play with words and live more poetically in the world. She is the author of *Pretty Things Please* (Turning Point, 2016). Two poems from this collection were featured on *The Writer's Almanac.* She has served as Poet-in-Residence in schools throughout New England and works as a psychotherapist.

Matthew Thorburn is the author of six books, including *String,* a novel in poems (LSU Press, 2023); *The Grace of Distance* (LSU Press, 2019), a finalist for the Paterson Poetry Prize; and the book-length poem *Dear Almost* (LSU Press, 2016), which won the Lascaux Prize. He lives in New Jersey.

Alison Townsend is the author of *The Green Hour: A Natural History of Home* and two books of poetry, *Persephone in America* and *The Blue Dress.* Her work has appeared in such journals as *Blackbird, The Southern Review,* and *The Kenyon Review,* and has been recognized in *Best American Poetry, The Pushcart Prize,* and *Best American Essays 2020.* She is Professor Emerita of English at the University of Wisconsin-Whitewater.

Rhett Iseman Trull is the author of *The Real Warnings* (Anhinga Press, 2009), which received the Brockman-Campbell Book Award, the Devil's Kitchen Reading Award, and the Oscar Arnold Young Award. Her poems have appeared in *32 Poems, American Poetry Review, Image,* and elsewhere. She is editor of *Cave Wall* and president of the Nina Riggs Poetry Foundation.

Maryfrances Wagner was Missouri's sixth Poet Laureate (2021–2023). Her most recent book is *Solving for X* (Spartan Press, 2022). She co-edits I-*70 Review* and serves on The Writers' Place board. Her poems have appeared in such journals as *New Letters, Laurel Review,* and *Rattle,* and in such anthologies as *Unsettling America: An Anthology of Contemporary Multicultural Poetry* (Penguin) and *Literature Across Cultures* (Pearson/Longman).

Elinor Ann Walker is the author of the chapbook, *Fugitive but Gorgeous,* which was selected as the winner of the 2024 Sheila-Na-Gig First Chapbook Contest (Sheila-Na-Gig Editions, 2025). She has published poems in *AGNI, Nimrod, Plume, The Southern Review,* and elsewhere. Her work has also been featured on *Verse Daily.*

Helen Wallace is the founder and curator of Poetry at the Dali Museum and former Poet Laureate of St. Petersburg, Florida. Her first book, *Shimming the Glass House* (Ashland Poetry Press, 2009), won the Richard Snyder Prize. Individual poems have been included in *Plume, Harvard Review, The Midwest Quarterly,* and elsewhere.

Michael Waters' books include *Pagan Sky: New & Selected Poems 2000–2025* (BOA Editions, 2026), *Sinnerman* (Etruscan, 2023), *Caw* (BOA, 2020), and two co-edited anthologies. His poems have appeared in *The Pushcart Prize* and *Best American Poetry* anthologies. Recipient of fellowships from the NEA, Guggenheim Foundation, and the Fulbright Foundation, he lives in New Jersey.

Laura Grace Weldon was Ohio's 2019 Poet of the Year and is the author of four books. She works as a book editor, teaches writing workshops, and serves as the *Braided Way* editor. Her background includes teaching nonviolence, leading abuse survivor support groups, and writing collaborative poetry with nursing home residents.

Ingrid Wendt has authored five books of poems and co-edited two poetry anthologies. Her poems have appeared in *Poetry, Terrain, About Place,* and elsewhere. Her honors include the Oregon Book Award, residencies at Hedgebrook and the Wurlitzer Foundation, and three features on Garrison Keillor's *The Writer's Almanac.*

Sarah Wetzel is the author of three poetry collections: *The Davids Inside David* (Terrapin Books, 2019), *River Electric with Light* (Red Hen Press, 2015), which won the AROHO Poetry Publication Prize, and *Bathsheba Transatlantic* (Anhinga Press, 2010). She is also the author of a chapbook, *Elegies of Herons* (Black Sunflowers Poetry Press). The publisher and editor at Saturnalia Books, she lives in New York City.

George Witte is the author of four poetry collections, most recently *An Abundance of Caution* (Unbound Edition Press, 2023). His poems have been published in such journals as *The Gettysburg Review, The Kenyon Review, Ploughshares,* and *Prairie Schooner,* and in several anthologies, including *The Best American Poetry* and *The Doll Collection* (Terrapin Books, 2016). He lives in New Jersey.

Cecilia Woloch is the author of six collections of poems and a novel. Her honors include fellowships from the Fulbright Foundation, NEA, CEC/ArtsLink International, and the California Arts Council, as well as a Pushcart Prize and inclusion in the *Best American Poetry* series. Born in Pennsylvania, raised in rural Kentucky, and currently based in Los Angeles, she has traveled the world as a writer and teacher.

Michael T. Young is the author of three full-length books, most recently *The Infinite Doctrine of Water* (Terrapin Books, 2018). His poetry has appeared in such journals as *Talking River Review, Valparaiso Poetry Review,* and *Vox Populi,* and has been featured on *Verse Daily* and *The Writer's Almanac.* Recipient of a fellowship from the New Jersey State Council on the Arts, and the Chaffin Poetry Award, he lives in New Jersey.

Claire Zoghb is the author of *Small House Breathing* (Quercus Review Press, 2009) and two chapbooks. She has published poems in *Bellevue Literary Review, Another Chicago Magazine,* and *Crab Creek Review,* and in the anthologies *Through a Child's Eyes: Poems and Stories About War* and *Eating Her Wedding Dress: A Collection of Clothing Poems* (Ragged Sky, 2009). A graphic designer, she lives in Connecticut.

Credits

Susan Aizenberg. "July at Rose Blumkin" from *Quiet City* (BkMk Press). Copyright © 2015 by Susan Aizenberg. Reprinted by permission of BkMk Press.

Nin Andrews. "The House." Copyright © 2020 by Nin Andrews. First published in *Green Mountains Review*. Reprinted by permission of the author.

Cheryl Baldi. "At First There Was No Air" from *Cormorants at Dusk* (Kelsay Books). Copyright © 2024 by Cheryl Baldi. Reprinted by permission of the author.

Tony Barnstone. "Parable of the Burning House" from *The Golem of Los Angeles* (Red Hen Press). Copyright © 2008 by Tony Barnstone. Reprinted by permission of the author.

Joseph Bathanti. "Entering an Abandoned House" from *Anson County* (Press 53). Copyright © 2013 by Joseph Bathanti. Reprinted by permission of the author.

Michele Battiste. "The 101st Note on Violence" (as "The Cook's Temptation") from *Waiting for the Wreck to Burn* (Trio House). Copyright © 2019 by Michele Battiste. Reprinted by permission of the author.

Jeanne Marie Beaumont. "Summer Ghazal" from *Lessons with Scissors* (Tiger Bark Press). Copyright © 2024 by Jeanne Marie Beaumont. Reprinted by permission of the author.

Regina Berg. "In My Mother's Last Garden." Copyright © 2023 by Regina Berg. First published in *The Bluebird Word*. Reprinted by permission of the author.

George Bilgere. "Zero" from *The White Museum* (Autumn House Press). Copyright © 2009 by George Bilgere. Reprinted by permission of the author.

Michelle Bitting. "No One Told Me About the Death." Copyright © 2021 by Michelle Bitting. First published in *Radar Poetry*. Reprinted by permission of the author.

Sally Bliumis-Dunn. "We Were Our Father's Second Family" from *Echolocation* (Plume Editions/MadHat Press). Copyright © 2018 by Sally Bliumis-Dunn. Reprinted by permission of the author.

Jody Bolz. "Threshold" from *The Near and Far* (Turning Point Books). Copyright © 2019 by Jody Bolz. Reprinted by permission of the author.

Laure-Anne Bosselaar. "I Needed for Months" from *Lately: New & Selected Poems* (Sungold Editions). Copyright © 2018 by Laure-Anne Bosselaar. Reprinted by permission of the author.

Alice Friman. "Depression Glass" from *On the Overnight Train: New and Selected Poems* (LSU). Copyright © 2024 by Alice Friman. Reprinted by permission of the author.

Timothy Geiger. "The Black House in White House Ohio" from *The Curse of Pheromones* (Main Street Rag Books). Copyright © 2008 by Timothy Geiger. Reprinted by permission of the author.

Maria Mazziotti Gillan. "The Little General" from *The Place I Call Home* (NYQ Books). Copyright © 2012 by Maria Mazziotti Gillan. Reprinted by permission of the author.

Jessica Goodfellow. "Torn." Copyright © 2022 by Jessica Goodfellow. First published in *Radar Poetry*. Reprinted by permission of the author.

Benjamin S. Grossberg. "Cricket in the House." Copyright © 2021 by Benjamin S. Grossberg. First published in *Prairie Schooner*. Reprinted by permission of the author.

Barbara Hamby. "Ode on Paradis and the Longing for a Place that Never Was" from *Burn* (University of Pittsburgh Press). Copyright © 2025 by Barbara Hamby. Reprinted by permission of the author.

Jeffrey Harrison. "Inauguration of a House" from *Incomplete Knowledge* (Four Way Books). Copyright © 2006 by Jeffrey Harrison. Reprinted with the permission of The Permissions Company, Inc. on behalf of Four Way Books.

Leslie Harrison. "[Things the realtor will not tell the new owner]" from *The Book of Endings* (University of Akron Press). Copyright © 2017 by Leslie Harrison. Reprinted by permission of the author.

Donna Hilbert. "Seventh Avenue North, Seattle" from *Gravity: New & Selected Poems* (Tebot Bach). Copyright © 2018 by Donna Hilbert. Reprinted by permission of the author.

Andrea Hollander. "Living Room" from *Landscape with Female Figure: New and Selected Poems: 1982–2012* (Autumn House Press). Copyright © 2013 by Andrea Hollander. Reprinted by permission of the author.

Alison Jarvis. "Ice Fishing, Lac Qui Parle" from *Where Is North* (Silverfish Review Press). Copyright © 2017 by Alison Jarvis. Reprinted by permission of the author.

Jeffrey N. Johnson. "Nine Month Lease." Copyright © 2010 by Jeffrey N. Johnson. First published in *Gargoyle*. Reprinted by permission of the author.

Tina Kelley. "When I Become Your House." Copyright © 2021 by Tina Kelley. First published in *The Hopkins Review*. Reprinted by permission of the author.

Adele Kenny. "Anything with Wings" from *Where Eternity Is Learned* (Welcome Rain). Copyright © 2025 by Adele Kenny. Reprinted by permission of the author.

187

About the Editor

Diane Lockward is the author of four poetry books, most recently *The Uneaten Carrots of Atonement* (Wind Publications, 2016). She is also the editor of *The Strategic Poet: Honing the Craft* and three previous craft books. Her awards include the Quentin R. Howard Poetry Prize, a poetry fellowship from the New Jersey State Council on the Arts, and a Woman of Achievement Award. Her poems have been included in such journals as the *Harvard Review, Southern Poetry Review,* and *Prairie Schooner.* Her work has also been featured on *Poetry Daily, Verse Daily,* Ted Kooser's *American Life in Poetry,* and Garrison Keillor's *The Writer's Almanac.* The founder and publisher of Terrapin Books, she lives in New Jersey.

www.ingramcontent.com/pod-product-compliance
Lightning Source LLC
Jackson TN
JSHW080354170225
78997JS00002B/5